Death in the Winter Solstice:
A Narrative of a True Murder Mystery in Homer

Copyright 2012 by Martin A. Sweeney

ISBN: 148026542X

Published by:
Cortland County Historical Society
25 Homer Avenue
Cortland, NY 13045
(607)756-6071
cortlandhistory@centralny.twcbc.com

Nestled on the corner of two side streets, resides the Cortland County Historical Society; home to the Kellogg Memorial Research Center and the Suggett House Museum. The Kellogg Memorial Research Center offers visitors the chance to explore the past of Cortland County and their families' relationship to it. With files on hundreds of families that have lived in Cortland, vital statistics (births, deaths, marriages) cut from the newspaper, a photograph collection numbering in the tens of thousands, articles archived by topic, diaries, letters, store ledgers, census records, maps and more those searching for their family or topics of interest in Cortland County are always bound to find something.

Visitors to the Suggett House Museum will revel in the number of items related to the History of Cortland County on display. The main exhibit, At Home, Historic Interiors of Cortland County showcases the history of the county by how residents would have lived during previous eras. The Military Room (located on the second floor) is one not to miss. Starting with the Spanish and American War, and continuing through Korea, the display highlights the role Cortland County Soldiers played in supporting our country. A special display pays tribute to Llewellyn P. Norton, of Scott (Cortland County), one of two Congressional Medal of Honor winners from Cortland County. Returning back to the first floor visitors then see a small exhibit on the Suggett Family, before entering the dining room, which serves as a changing exhibit room. After this you are ushered into the kitchen which could come right out of any 19th century home.

Contents

Introduction

If shows like *Castle, CSI, NCIS,* or *Law and Order* are any indicator, people love a good murder mystery. The thrill of trying to crack the case open, along side the television detectives, takes us on a ride unlike any other. In *Death in the Winter Solstice: A Narrative of a True Murder Mystery in Homer,* Homer Town Historian, Martin Sweeney (author of *Lincoln's Gift from Homer, New York: A Painter, an Editor, and a Detective*), takes the reader along for that same ride. From the beginning the readers find themselves engaged in this true story of murder in the late 19th century, farm town of Homer, New York.

As director of Cortland County Historical Society it is my privilege to congratulate Martin on a job well down and thank him for contributing this murder mystery to the publications of Cortland County Historical Society.

I hope that you enjoy this book as much as I have.

Sincerely,

Mindy A. Leisenring

Mindy A. Leisenring

CCHS Director

Death in the Winter Solstice:
A Narrative of a True Murder Mystery in Homer

Preface

Fortunately, since its creation in April of 1808, Cortland County, in the heart of New York State, has experienced within its mostly rural borders a minimal amount of homicidal activity. Records indicate that the number of murders since 1843 have numbered about fifty-seven. Of course, even one is too many. The earliest on record was in 1843 in Virgil when Lydia Edwards killed her 76 year old father, Jonathan Edwards. It was brutal. She struck the man several times with an axe and then took the man's razor and slit his throat. She claimed she planned to take her mother's life, too, and then her own. Lydia was sent to the Lunatic Asylum in Utica. Only one execution for the conviction of murder has ever occurred in the county. Patrick O'Donaghue of Truxton was hanged in the Cortland courthouse [not the current county courthouse] in August of 1853 for a double murder. On September 3, 1852, he clubbed to death Amanda Jane Kinney and her 12 year old daughter, Jane Kinney, when he thought the Kinneys were responsible for the disappearance of his own daughter. In more recent years, the newspapers reported the deaths of two women -- Wendy Thibeault in 2009 and Janet Pottorff in 2012. In each case, the husband was arrested for murder, and one is now doing time in state prison.

And then there is the mysterious case of the bludgeoning death of Patrick Quinlan of Homer, New York, on December 22, 1894.

The Quinlan case was originally the subject of a series of installments that started running in *The Homer News* in 2010. In response to some of the readers who asked that the installments be published as a book, I offered the manuscript, with some changes made, to the Cortland County Historical Society for publication. All proceeds from the sale of the book go to benefit the work done by the Society, of which I am a member, and for its maintenance of the Suggett House museum on Homer Avenue, Cortland, NY.

This narrative was fashioned from accounts reported in *The Cortland Evening Standard* from 1894-95, which are available on microfilm at the Cortland Public Library. Additional sources used were: *Parsons' Directory of Cortland County, New York,* for 1894 and one file on "Hangings" and another on "Murders" (all available at the Cortland County Historical Society); the federal census records of 1880, 1890, 1900, and 1910 (available online); and research material compiled by the late municipal historian R. Curtis Harris in the 1960s (in Town of Homer archives). No names or locations have been changed. Present day locations of past events have been parenthetically provided the reader, where known. The dialogue is based upon the material presented by reporters of the day who observed the trial, but some liberties were taken to give the plot and characters involved some humanity and color. The primary sources provided physical descriptions of only the murder victim. With only a few exceptions, I avoided the temptation of using fictive descriptions of the other people. Because of the historian in me, accuracy trumped creativity. Instead, I chose to let the dialogue feed the reader's imagination.

I wish to acknowledge the help I received from the staff of the Cortland Public Library; from Mindy Leisenring, Director of the Cortland County Historical Society; from Jeremy Boylan, Cortland County Historian; and from Anita Jebbett, the Homer Town Clerk, who always is willing to provide information to help in matching places of the past with present day homes and businesses in Homer. My gratitude is extended to Mindy Leisenring and Professor Len Ralston for the careful editing provided. In addition, Mindy must be acknowledged for the time put into the gathering of illustrations from various sources and doing the layout. Finally, a special word of appreciation goes to my artist friend David Quinlan for providing information on the murder case, for designing the evocative cover for the book, and for his continual support of my feeble attempts at researching and writing local history. He is one of the several friends of Historic Homer who unceasingly advocate for Homer's rightful place in "heritage tourism" in Central New York.

For David and all you sleuths who enjoy a good opportunity to determine "who done it," this narrative is dedicated to you. See if you can identify the most likely suspect. Who killed Homer's Patrick Quinlan in 1894?

Martin A. Sweeney
Town of Homer Historian
Author of *Lincoln's Gift from Homer, New York*

October 5, 2012

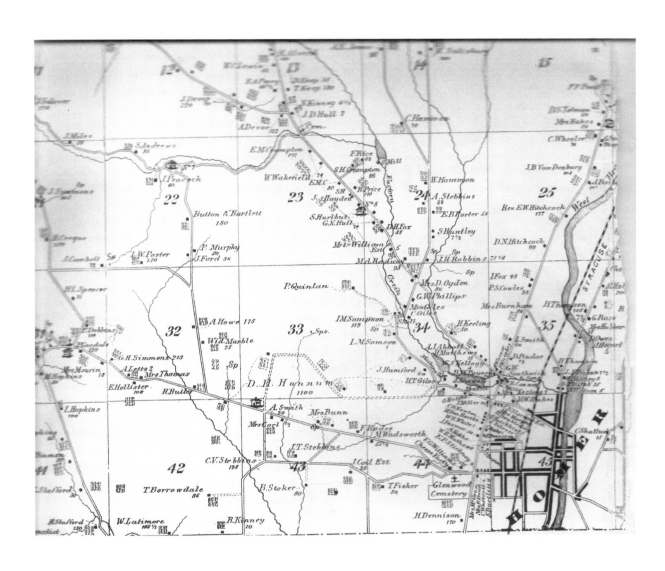

1

The Longest Night of the Year

Dec. 21, 1894:

"Aye, with Christmas a comin,' 'tis a wondrous feelin'."

Patrick Quinlan stood at the wooden bar at Doyle's Pub at the Central Hotel at No.4 North Main Street [now Dasher's Corner Pub] in the village of Homer, New York. He was feeling hale and hearty. Christmas 1894 was only four days away, and he was basking in the admiration poured on him by another patron in response to his

boasting of good fortune. He had received a tidy sum for the sale of Christmas turkeys. Earlier in the day, he had come into the village to the Brockway Block on Main Street and sold the fowl for $40.57 to O. B. Andrews & Company [present site of Homer History Center at Key Bank]. Now, he had come back to town for a much needed pre-holiday haircut at Bill Jones' barbershop at 13 James Street and to savor a drink or two at Doyle's place on the corner.

After quaffing a glass of dark beer he made his way over to another room, Doyle's office. John Doyle, pulling slowly at his moustache, was seated at his big wooden desk, with other men standing or seated nearby. Quinlan pulled up a wooden chair and plunked down his six-foot, two hundred pound frame as he heard the saloonkeeper remark something about it being a good time to be selling cabbage. The men in the social gathering were either hard-working laborers or, like Quinlan, dairy farmers from the area. The former found employment making carriages and wagons at either Brockway's Wagon Company at the south end of Main Street or the Homer Manufacturing Company on James Street (which incorporated in 1895 as the Homer Wagon Company). Their accents meant that the majority could trace their origins back to Ireland, having come to the States around the time of the Great Famine or later. The struggles of life had taught these men to work hard and to play hard and to raise more than *praties* [potatoes] for a living.

Patrick Quinlan entered into the pleasant conversation, but after ten minutes he

First Decade of the 20th Century

took out his pocket watch, glanced at the time, and announced it was time to be going home. Stopping at the bar, he ordered another glass of beer, downed it quickly, pulled a woolen hat onto his graying head, and went out the back door into the cool air of the first night of winter. It was the winter solstice – the moment when the earth's axial tilt would be the furthest away from the Sun. This was to be the longest night of the year. Two other men, in their twenties, immediately left the bar by the front door and stepped out into the silence of Main Street. Illuminated by the modern, electric arc street lamps installed three years earlier, the sixty-four year old Quinlan trudged alone up James Street past Skahan's blacksmith shop [19 James St.] toward the railroad tracks and the train depot [now offices of the Homer Village Police Department].

James Street, Homer, NY Today

D. L. and W. R. R. Station, Homer, N. Y.

He was heading on foot in the direction of his prosperous two hundred acre dairy farm that was a couple miles northwest of the village. As he had done countless times before by foot and by horse-pulled wagon, he made his way up the main road that led to Scott and then turned onto the lane that cut across his property, known on the Town records as Lots 33 and 34. At that point he was half a mile from his hillside farmhouse door with a stretch of ground before him that seemed desolate even in daylight. No wife was waiting to greet him; he was a widower. His wife had died fifteen years ago, leaving him with a daughter and a son. Julia, 34 years old and unmarried, had assumed her mother's domestic burdens, and 31 year old Thomas, also unmarried, helped his father with the farm chores. As cradle Catholics, the Quinlans drove into Cortland every Sunday for Mass at St. Mary's [located where St. Mary's School is today]. It would be another fifteen years before the devout of Homer would have a parish church of their own named after pious Saint Margaret, 11th century Queen of Scotland. By all appearances, matters of the sod and of the soul were the family's main preoccupations, and an occasional tippling on a Friday night like this one was viewed by Patrick as one of the few pleasures left to him in this world. So, with only the moon to light his way and the alcohol in his blood to warm him, he made his way past the village limits -- beyond the houses with their doors hung with evergreens and their windows aglow with tinseled Christmas trees. It was one of those moments where it felt good to be alive. God's in His Heaven, and all's well with the world.

. . . .

Dec. 22, 1894:

"I found him this morning lyin' face down in the road."

John Doyle could not believe what Thomas Quinlan was telling him. The saloonkeeper had just finished his Saturday mid-day dinner when the distraught son of Patrick Quinlan entered the hotel and began quizzing him.

"Was my father here last night?"

"That he was, Tom."

"Was he drinkin' anything?"

"He did," replied Doyle, who sensed something was wrong.

"How much?" probed the young farmer, with worry in his voice.

"Two or three glasses of beer" was the answer, followed by a question from the concerned saloonkeeper: "Has he got home yet?"

"He has. I found him in the road this morning when I was comin' down with the milk. He was lyin' face down. I rolled him over, and he had a terribly black eye. I could not get him to come to."

Doyle grimaced at the image in his mind.

Quinlan continued, "We haven't been able to rouse him yet, so I've come into town for Dr. White." And then the son returned to questioning: "Did my father stop at any other place last night that you know of?"

Doyle answered that he did not know. Then he asked Thomas to explain again how he had come upon his father.

"I was comin' down with the milk, and I saw him lyin' face down in the lane about half way between our house and the main road. He was breathin' loudly, like snorin'. I assumed he was drunk and had been out with the boys last night. Since it weren't that cold, around 40 degrees, I thought it best to let him sleep it off while I drove to town, delivered the milk at the depot, bought some bread at the bakery, and

8

then drove back home. On the way to the house, I stopped and managed to get him into the wagon and carried him to the house."

"I have to tell you, Tom," replied Doyle, stroking his moustache, "this doesn't sound like your father. I've known your father for a long time and I never saw the man drunk but once. Stone drunk is not like him at all."

"I know," agreed Thomas. "I've got to get back; I want to be there when the doctor arrives."

As he left, Doyle was running the story through his mind again and again. Something did not make sense here.

Later, at the onset of night, Doc White's son called with disconcerting news, "Father's back from Mr. Quinlan's. He says that Mr. Quinlan's skull was broken in and he's not expected to live." Immediately, Doyle called Officer Porter, and the two of them went to Doctor White's office at 21 Cayuga Street to get his assessment of Quinlan's condition. From there, they drove directly to the Quinlan house. Arriving around 6 in the evening, they were met at the door by Mrs. Lucy, a friend of the Quinlans, and by the daughter, Julia, with a face stained with tears. Doyle looked around. He could see Patrick Quinlan lying in his bed in a room off from the sitting room. He was unconscious. His son was nowhere to be seen.

2

"It's a terrible thing."

The Homer saloonkeeper turned his gaze from the still form of Patrick Quinlan and fixed upon the man's daughter.

"Where's Tom?" Doyle asked Julia.

"He's gone for Father John."

And with that she began sobbing again. Mrs. Lucy got her seated upon a settee and attempted to comfort her.

"Julia," said Doyle as he sat beside her and took her left hand in his. "I want you to try and tell Officer Porter what happened."

Sobbing renewed.

"It's a terrible thing," was all she could manage to get out between sobs.

Doyle offered her his linen handkerchief, and when she settled down again he asked, "Where was Tom last night? Did he go into town, too?"

Officer Porter listened carefully as Julia explained that Tom had not gone into town last night. She and her brother had retired early to their separate rooms upstairs.

"What time did your father leave last night for the village?"

"Sometime between six and seven o'clock."

Doyle and Officer Porter did not remain much longer. Instead, with a lantern in hand, they decided to go down to the place where Patrick Quinlan had been found. In the darkness, they poked around squinting at the ground . Porter found a stick or part of a fence post, but they admitted that there was no certainty that they were in the exact spot where the old farmer had been found. Leaving the stick there and deciding it was too dark to get a good look at anything, they returned to town.

Both men were at Doyle's at 11 PM when Thomas Quinlan stopped in. He

Barn of Cortland-Homer Horse R.R, Co. ~1882

declined a drink, explaining that he was returning from Cortland and had some brandy and arnica[1] which he had been told to fetch to put on his father's tongue with the hope that it might cause him to rally. Doyle said he would probably stop at the farmhouse in the morning to see how Patrick was faring. Thomas offered his thanks and headed out the back door.

"God be with you and with your father," he heard Doyle say as he departed.

Dec. 23, 1894:

The next day was Sunday, December 23. Doc White returned that evening to the bedside of Patrick Quinlan accompanied by Dr. Higgins of Cortland and Dr. Robinson of Homer [35 South Main]. They found Quinlan, as he had been, unconscious and breathing heavily. The doctors examined the contused wound on the front side of the old man's head above his right ear. They agreed the best they could do under the circumstances was to perform a bit of surgery. Removing the pieces of bone that were impacting the brain might reduce pressure on the brain. Perhaps the man might regain consciousness for a long enough period to shed some light on the mystery. Dr. Higgins, assisted by the other two physicians, proceeded to carefully remove a tri-cornered fragment of the skull two inches in length and one and a half inches in width. They also managed to remove a quantity of clotted blood from the brain. Once the delicate procedure was done, they waited and watched. They knew it was hopeless. There were other clots of blood pressing against the brain which were simply impossible to

---

[1] Arnica is an herb related to the sunflower that was believed to have medicinal value.

remove. The old man's breathing became increasingly shallow over the next half hour. They summoned his children to the deathbed. At 7:15 PM, the evening before Christmas Eve, Patrick Quinlan breathed his last.

The physicians agreed that the Coroner needed to be notified. It was not an unattended death, but an autopsy, under the circumstances, would be needed. In their opinion, death had been caused by a compression of the brain produced by injuries inflicted upon the head by some object in the hands of some person other than the old man himself. Clearly, in their opinion, Patrick Quinlan had been murdered.

Dec. 24, 1894:

The day of Christmas Eve, 1894, meant last minute holiday preparations for the folks of Cortland County, but the Quinlan Case meant no break for the law enforcement personnel of the county. The Coroner was summoned, and in the early afternoon Sheriff Miller and District Attorney Jerome Squires were on the scene to begin an investigation.

Dr. George Bradford, respected Homer physician and descendant of the illustrious William Bradford of the *Mayflower* and Plimouth Plantation, was the Coroner for Homer. As such, he knew an inquest was in order to determine the cause of Patrick Quinlan's death. He drew as an inquest jury Hugh McDermott as foreman to be joined by William C. Collins, E. Bockes, William Foster, Byron Maxson, Warren Clark, Charles H. Danes, Harmon Hooker, and George Eldridge. He had the nine men view the remains and then adjourned until Wednesday morning, the day after Christmas.

Meanwhile, on that Monday, the 24th of December, an autopsy was conducted at the farmhouse by Dr. Frank W. Green of 4 Pine Street and Dr. John W. Whitney of 50 North Main. They examined the stomach and found no traces of alcohol. All of the internal organs were in a perfectly healthy condition. They determined that the deceased had not been a hard drinker. They concluded that very powerful blows had to have been inflicted to break the heavy bones of the skull in the way in which it was done. The hat which the old man had worn was badly torn and contained blood. Another wound was discovered, which they reported "looked as though it was caused by a blow from a sand bag, as there were no external indications, but its results showed underneath the bones." This wound was on the back of the head, which they offered as evidence that more than one person was involved. Such a blow to the back of the head would have been sufficient to cause insensibility.

The Sheriff and the DA arrived at the site of the alleged assault accompanied by a reporter from *The Cortland Evening Standard* and a Cortland attorney, Thomas E. Courtney. In their presence, Thomas Quinlan was questioned at length. He explained that he did the chores Friday evening as usual at about six o'clock. He went to bed early, and his sister did, also, but they left the door unbolted for their father.

"And in the morning? When you found he had not returned, what did you think?" asked District Attorney Squires.

"We didn't worry," responded Thomas. "We supposed Pa had spent the night with his brother, who lives above Brewery Hill [above Albany Street]. That was something he had done before when he was detained in Homer."

"Where did you discover the body?" inquired the DA.

"Over here," answered Thomas, pointing in the direction of a small tree at the right side of the road going up the hill. "He was lying by the tree."

"And was there any indication he'd been robbed?"

"In the road was his jack knife and a plug of tobacco, and his pockets had been rifled. There was no money in his pockets. And some nails that he'd been carryin' in his pocket were scattered in the road."

"Anything else you remember?" asked the sheriff, who was nosing about the site.

"Yes, Pa's belt had been torn from his waist."

The sheriff bent down and picked up what appeared to be a fence post. He examined it closely.

"This may have been used in the assault," opined the sheriff as he squinted at marks that looked like bloodstains along the surface of the post he was holding.

13

The DA asked how much money Thomas supposed was stolen.

"I don't know, but Pa always carried between fifteen and thirty dollars on him, and he had received the day before a milk check for about fifty dollars. I think he turned forty dollars over to Julia for her turkeys he sold to the grocer. I know he had recently drawn money from a certificate of deposit at the bank and used $8.50 to purchase two blankets. But I have no idea how much he carried on him when this happened."

"Tell me, again, your father's condition when you first came upon him," said the DA, who was trying to mentally reconstruct the crime scene.

"Like I told you on the phone yesterday, I found Pa lying face downward with his head on his hands. When I couldn't rouse him, I turned him over. And his face was in a pool of blood. He was soaked with it. I could see he had been bleeding from his nose and ears."

"And what did you do next?"

"I took Pa to the house."

"You turned the wagon around and took your father to the house?" asked the reporter, who had been looking around unsuccessfully trying to locate any tracks from where the team and wagon had been turned around.

Thomas seemed hesitant in answering. Sheepishly, with eyes down, he replied, "Well…to tell the truth…I did not."

The members of the investigation team looked at each other. The reporter snapped back, "I understand that you told the DA yesterday that you did."

"I know I said so, but that was not so."

"So what did happen?" probed the reporter, with pencil ready to apply to a notebook.

"I thought Pa was drunk. So I took the milk to Homer, and when I returned I placed him in the wagon and took him home." The men eyed each other.

"You did all of this by yourself? Got a heavy man in and out of the wagon by yourself?" questioned the reporter.

Thomas was now becoming defensive. "Look, I had considerable difficulty. I managed to drag Pa to the wagon and to lift him in…"

"Without help?" the reporter interjected.

"Yes. I only managed to get him into the wagon because Pa's legs were rigid, from having lain there all night, I suppose. And my sister helped me to get him into the house. We undressed him and got him onto his bed. Then we bathed him and rubbed his legs and feet 'til they were warm."

"Why didn't you notify someone immediately?" asked the sheriff.

"I supposed Pa had fallen down in a drunken stupor and injured his head and would come to."

"You didn't think his injury was serious?" joined in the DA.

"Well, of course. By mid-day dinner we got really worried because he wasn't coming to."

"And it was another four hours before he was seen by Doc White. Why so long?" the reporter asked incredulously.

"Now listen here," retorted Thomas, "when Pa was still unconscious after dinner, I drove into town and arrived at Doc White's at about 1 o'clock. He had an office full of patients. It was his office hours, and he told me it would be two hours -- at least two hours – before he would be able to get away. I told him he had to come as soon as he could, and I guess it was sometime after 3 o'clock when he started."

"Did your father ever regain consciousness?" asked Attorney Courtney.

"No, never. Doc dressed his wound, told us he didn't think Pa had long to live. I called Father McLoughlin, drove to Cortland, and brought him back. He gave Pa extreme unction and remained with him part of the night. Pa never came around, and I want those responsible held accountable."

Thomas turned on his heels and walked back up the lane to do his daily chores.

3

The Coroner's Inquest

Dec. 26, 1894:

On December 26, The Cortland Evening Standard reported that "Christmas brought no new light upon the Quinlan murder." It was also reported that "Thomas Quinlan, the murdered man's son, in an interview with a STANDARD reporter on Monday deviated somewhat from the story he had previously told." Readers were briefly given the discrepancies in Thomas' two accounts of how soon he had tended to his father on the day after what the newspaper had called "a Dastardly Crime." Reporting a "murderous assault" with robbery "doubtless the motive" was bound to agitate a community, and knowledge that the unknown assailant was still at large and might be in their midst elevated their level of concern.

The sun of the recent solstice rose radiantly on that crisp and clear morning of Wednesday, December 26. While the devout had attended church services in Homer and Cortland the day before, the Quinlans had not been among them, and many a conversation at Christmas tables had included conjectures about what had transpired on last Friday evening. At 9 o'clock on this day after Christmas, an undertaker took the remains of Patrick Quinlan by a horse-pulled black hearse to Pompey Hill in the southeast part of nearby Onondaga County. There, Mass was offered, and Patrick was buried beside the grave of his beloved wife who had passed on fifteen years earlier.

Forty minutes later, in Homer, the coroner's inquest in the Quinlan case was officially opened. The whole number of jurymen selected was assembled in the wainscoted office of Coroner Bradford. This was in the six year old Brockway Block on Main Street that also housed O. B. Andrews' grocery store.

The first witness called to the stand was Dr. Green, practicing physician in Homer. Dr. Green testified that he had been called to make a post mortem examination of the body of Patrick Quinlan on Monday, December 24. Dr. Green explained, "I found the body in the parlor of the residence of the deceased. The clothing had been removed, and the body of a man between sixty and seventy years of age was exposed. I found no external marks of violence on the body, only on the head and face."

When asked to describe the actual autopsy and his findings, the doctor gave this graphic statement, which was not meant for the squeamish: "I first opened the thorax and abdominal cavities and examined the internal organs. I found them all in healthy condition. Then, I examined the head. There was a discoloration over the right eye, extending down to the nose, which was broken. The discoloration was three inches in diameter. The temporal bones on the right side of the head were crushed. There was an opening in the right side of the skull two inches above the ear and about two inches by three-quarters of an inch extending into the temporal bone and nearly to the frontal. The line of fracture extended from the opening about two and one-half inches downward and backward. Another fracture followed into the orbital plate. There was another line of fracture extending along the right side of the skull, near the vertex extending from the frontal backward to the occipital bone. Next, I removed the skull cap. I found a large clot of blood under the right parietal bone between that and the covering over the right lobe of the brain. This clot also extended back to the base of the brain. A hemorrhage was also formed at the side of the brain."

Although some of those present found the doctor's detailed professional assessment a bit unsettling, the doctor forged on: "I knew the decedent in life by sight only. I am prepared to affirm, from the examination I made, that death resulted from the wounds which had the appearance of being inflicted by powerful blows upon the head and that there seemed to have been at least three blows. One appeared to have been received over the right eye and the bridge of the nose. Another blow seems to have been received on the right side of the head. This blow was above the ear and was one of the most powerful ones received. Only upon removing the scalp was the blow at the back of the head discovered. This was discovered by the large clot of blood which I found between the skull and the scalp. These were the only evidences I discovered."

Then, the doctor was asked if such injuries as he described could have been received from a fall.

"No," he responded, "in my opinion, death was caused due to the man having received three blows which caused hemorrhages on the structure of the brain and the shock to the structure of the head."

Upon further questioning by the jury the doctor declared that there was no break of the skin on the body; there was no evidence in the organs to prove that the man was drunk at the time of his death; and the right eye was filled with blood.

Dr. Whitney of Homer was the next witness. He stated that he, too, had been called upon by the coroner to examine the body said to be that of the late Patrick Quinlan, and that he made such examination on December 24, 1894, at the home of the deceased. Continuing, the doctor's testimony corroborated that made by Dr. Green, with just a few exceptions. He stated that the left eye was also slightly discolored and that there was no hemorrhage on the brain but merely a slight concussion. He, also, added, "In my opinion, the blow on the eye and nose might have been struck after the man had fallen, but in no way was it received by a fall. The first blow received was to the top of the head and it was sufficient to render the man unconscious."

Dr. White was the next witness, but his testimony was interrupted at noon and the inquest was adjourned until 2 PM. At that time, Coroner Bradford had the doctor return to the stand, but the coroner requested the press to refrain from publishing his testimony "for the present" since it might hinder the efforts of "those who are seeking for the murderer."

Mr. E. H. Knapp followed Dr. White on the witness stand. Knapp identified himself as the manager of the Homer milk depot[2] and that Patrick Quinlan was one of his patrons. He gave a straightforward response to a line of questioning.

"Mr. Quinlan himself was in the habit of coming to the depot with the milk," he stated, "but on Saturday morning, December 22, 1894, Thomas Quinlan brought the milk to the depot."

"Do you remember the time?"

"It was the usual time…between 8 and 8:30 AM."

"Did Thomas Quinlan come to the depot the next day?"

"Yes, he came on Sunday morning."

"Did he say anything either time about his father?"

"As I recall, he said nothing about his father the first morning, but on Sunday morning, when I asked how his father was doing, because I had heard about the incident, he said his father was unconscious and not expected to be any better."

"Did he say anything more about the incident?"

"Only where he found his father."

"Is it true, Mr. Knapp, that you gave Mr. Patrick Quinlan a check on December 20th?"

"That I did," Knapp responded, "in the amount of $40.17."

A black man, referred to by The Cortland Evening Standard in the vernacular of the day as "colored," took the stand next. He was William A. Jones, local barber. He confirmed that Patrick Quinlan had come into his shop last Friday evening and had his hair cut and that he was not intoxicated at the time.

Augustus H. Bennett, resident of 13 Clinton Street and cashier at the Homer National Bank, then testified as to banking transactions of the decedent. He stated that

---

[2] Homer had two milk stations in 1894: One on the west side of Maple Avenue and another on the north side of Cayuga Street at the railroad crossing, just east of the tracks.

on December 14th Patrick Quinlan received $50 on a certificate of deposit. On December 20th Quinlan received $40.17 cash on a milk check. On December 21st Quinlan cashed a poultry check for $40.59.

Then, Thomas V. Martin was called to offer testimony as to when he had last seen Patrick Quinlan.

"I last saw him at Doyle's hotel on Friday evening, December 21st. Quinlan came in after I did. He, Doyle, and I were in the barroom alone. He was only there about fifteen minutes, I think. He said that it was time he was going home. I started out the front door, and Quinlan followed me, but I never saw him after that."

The last to testify in the inquest was Joseph D. Pratt of 9 William Street and the proprietor of The Ink Stand saloon in Homer [location undetermined]. He was asked when and where he had last seen Patrick Quinlan.

"I last saw him Friday evening, December 21st, at a little after 7 o'clock. He was going west toward the railroad tracks on James Street."

"Was he acting like he was drunk?"

"No, I thought he had been drinking, but he was not intoxicated."

At the conclusion of Pratt's testimony, Coroner Bradford suddenly held up a hat and overcoat and announced, "These are the garments worn by Patrick Quinlan when his body was discovered." The hat was torn. The coat was daubed with mud. Both were covered with blood stains. After the jury members had had a chance to thoroughly inspect the clothing, Coroner Bradford announced, "This inquest stands adjourned until nine o'clock on Monday morning, December 31st."

4

Proprietor of Doyle's Pub Testifies

Dec. 31, 1894:

Several witnesses took the stand on the last day of the year 1894. The coroner's inquest resumed at 9:30 A.M. with intent to establish the whereabouts of several parties on the night of Patrick Quinlan's death.

"John Doyle, when and where did you last see Patrick Quinlan alive?" Bradford asked.

The saloonkeeper responded, "I last saw him in the barroom of my place, the Central Hotel, on Friday evening, December 21st."

"Can you recall the time?"

"About 8 o'clock."

"How long was he there?"

"About half an hour."

"During that time were other individuals in the room?"

"Yes, other men came into the room."

"Can you name them now?"

Doyle tugged at the end of his moustache and proceeded to recall that eight men had been in the room that night: Tom Dane, Jack McDonald, Will Clark, John Bennett, Will Butler, George Rood, Alexander Stuart, and Tom Martin.

"Was Mr. Quinlan drinking?"

"He had a glass of beer."

"Did he have anything to say while at the bar?"

Doyle thought for a moment and then replied, "He talked about some turkeys he had brought to O. B. Andrews that day for which he received about forty dollars."

"Was he intoxicated?"

"No."

"Was anyone drinking with him?"

"No, no one was drinking with him. Will Butler and George Rood were standing at the other end of the bar eating, when Quinlan was drinking his beer, but no one drank with him."

"Who besides you heard him talk about the turkey money?"

"Tom Martin was the only one in the barroom then; the others were in my office."

"What happened after Mr. Quinlan finished his beer?"

"After drinking, Quinlan came out from the bar and sat down in the office."

"Did Mr. Quinlan talk about money then?"

"No, as I recall, there was no conversation about money, other than I said something about it being a good time to sell cabbage."

"Did Mr. Quinlan say anything about his coming into town by wagon or on foot?"

"Not that I can remember."

"What time did he leave?"

"Sometime after 8 o'clock he said it was time to go home. And after getting a second glass of beer, he went out the back door."

"Did anyone leave with him?"

"Jack McDonald and Louis Clark left by the front door when Quinlan went out the back door."

"At the same time Quinlan left the barroom?"

"Yes."

"Do you recall who left next?"

"Yes, John Bennett went out soon after."

"Was Patrick Quinlan sober when you saw him leave?"

"Yes."

"When did you first learn of Mr. Quinlan's injury?"

"Not until the next afternoon when Thomas Quinlan came in asking if his father had been drinking at the hotel on Friday night."

"Did he describe his father's injury?"

"All he said was that his father had a terribly black eye and was unconscious and that he had come to town for Dr. White."

"Did he say he was the first to come upon his father lying unconscious in their lane?"

"That he did. He said he was bringin' the milk to town when he found him."

"Did he say that he stopped and tended to his father then?"

"No, he said that he continued to bring the milk to town, to buy some bread at the bakery, and then to return home. He said he stopped on the way back to put his father in the wagon and take him home."

"Did he say why he did not stop while on his way to town to pick up his father?"

"He said he thought his father was snorin' and had passed out from drinkin' too much in town."

"What was your response to this?"

"I couldn't believe this had happened. I told Thomas that I only saw his father drunk once, and that was not that Friday night."

"How long, Mr. Doyle, have you known the Quinlan family?"

"Since I was a wee lad."

"And did you ever know of any quarreling among the members of the Quinlan family?"

"No, sir, never."

Doyle went on to tell of first learning of Quinlan's serious head injury from a call from Dr. White's son at dark that Saturday. He testified about accompanying Officer Porter out to the Quinlan Farm, of finding Quinlan unconscious, of looking over the spot where Quinlan had been found, and of Thomas Quinlan's visit to his hotel around 11 P.M.

"He was returnin' from Cortland with some brandy and arnica which the doctor or the priest had told him to get for his father," stated Doyle.

"When did you next see Thomas Quinlan?"

"The next day. I went out to the farm Sunday morning. Thomas was there, but I did not get to talk with him. I went back to the spot where Patrick was found to get a look in daylight."

"Did you see Thomas Quinlan any time after that?"

"Yes, I saw him on Thursday, after he returned from his father's funeral."

"What did he have to say to you?"

"He was upset with the newspapers. He told me that the newspapers had given him a bad reputation. He said that it was bad enough to have the trouble he had then without having the papers attack him. He said he planned to hire a detective to find the guilty parties if it took every cent he had."

The line of questioning then turned to John "Jack" McDonald, one of Doyle's patrons the night Patrick Quinlan was last seen at the bar.

"When was the next time you saw Mr. McDonald?"

"He was in my hotel with Mel Chapman on Christmas night."

"Can you recall conversing with him?"

"Yes. He told me that he understood that people were accusing him of the deal."

"By 'deal' he meant the injuries sustained by Patrick Quinlan?"

"Yes, and Jack said that when he left the Central Hotel on Friday night he went over to The Brunswick across the street and stayed all the rest of the evening. He said that Louis Clark was there with him."

Coroner Bradford then produced a stick and asked Doyle if this was the object he and Officer Porter had found when they visited the Quinlan farm. The witness said that it was. Doyle closed his testimony by confirming that several people had spoken to him of their suspicions that McDonald "had something to do with the deal."

Main St., Homer, N. Y.

Before Paving - About 1908 Wheadon, Bank, + Brockway Blo

Michael Murphy, proprietor of the Homer House at 33 South Main, was the next witness. He testified that he had known Patrick Quinlan since childhood.

"When did you last see Mr. Quinlan?" began the coroner.

"I saw him on Friday going up Main Street. He was opposite Dr. Webb's residence."

"You would be referring to Doctor Sumner Webb of 12 North Main Street?"

"Yes."

"Was Mr. Quinlan alone?"
"Yes."

"And when did you see him before that Friday night?"

"I am not sure. It may have been the previous Saturday night."

"Do you know a Mr. John McDonald and his line of work?"

"I do. He used to board at my place. He was a moulder in the employ of Charles Stone [iron foundry and machine shop at the corner of South Main and Copeland Avenue in Homer]."

"What do you mean 'he used to board' at your place?"

"He stopped boarding there last night."

All ears in the room perked up at this piece of information.

"Why is that, Mr. Murphy?"

"I've received but one week's rent from him," replied the irate landlord and owner of another establishment frequented by those seeking spirits and ales.

"When did you last have contact with Mr. McDonald?"

"That would be last night. He was in my saloon for the last time when he came to his supper with another boarder, Fred Graham."

"Did the two of you talk?"

"Yes. McDonald said that they had him 'put down for it,' meaning the unfortunate incident with Patrick Quinlan."

"And where were you on Friday evening, December 21st?"

"I was in my saloon," Murphy answered

"Did you see Mr. McDonald there?"

"I did, around 6:30 P.M., when I went out. I left Johnnie Connors in charge while I went to see Eva Tanquey in her show at the Opera House [third floor of the Keator Block, formerly known as the Barber Block, on Main Street]."

"Do you know if Mr. McDonald stayed at your establishment through the night of the 21st?"

"I have no way of knowing."

"Was Mr. Patrick Quinlan in the habit of coming to your place mornings?"

"I don't know. I am not usually the one tending to things mornings."

"Did you see Mr. McDonald on the morning of December 22nd?"

"I saw him, but I had no conversation with him."

"Have you seen him since then at your place?"

"He's come in almost every evening since."

"So you told Mr. McDonald that he better find another place to board?"

"I did, and he left this morning. He said he was going to his sister's in Cortland."

"I have one last question, Mr. Murphy. Can you recall hearing any of the conversation between Mr. McDonald and Mr. Graham last night?"

"Not much…other than they were laughing about their havin' been caught in a wire fence back of the academy on the Green one evening."

"Did you catch when this incident occurred?"

"No."

The witness was excused, and Nelson Crance was the next to be sworn in. He stated that his home was in Cortland and that he was employed at The Brunswick in Homer [second floor of the Keator Block; owned by Charles H. Healey; with a billiard parlor attached]. He stated that he was in The Brunswick on Friday, December 21st, from 7 A.M. to 11:30 P.M. He stated that he knew John McDonald but not Louis Clark.

"Was Mr. McDonald in the saloon that day or night?"

"Yes, he was there."

"Which -- daytime or evening?"

Crance could not recall, only that McDonald was there "only a few minutes."

"Did you have any conversation with him at that time?"

"I don't think so."

"Was he accompanied by anyone at that time?"

"I seem to recall there being a stranger with him -- a tall man he was, with a smooth face, about 28 years old, and he was dressed in dark clothes."

"Were they drinking?"

Crance smiled and explained, "They stepped up to the bar for drinks, but they didn't get any. They didn't have no money. They asked me if they was good for the drinks, and I told 'em they were not."

"Do you know a Mr. Will Butler?"

"I do."

"Was he in the saloon the evening of the 21st?"

"I...I...I'm sorry; I can't remember."

"Have you had any conversation with Mr. McDonald since the 21st?"

"Yes, I seen him one evening the first of last week. He came in and asked me if I remembered what time he had been there on December 21st."

"And what did you say?"

"I told him I couldn't remember. You see, my memory is none too good," Crance apologized.

"What did Mr. McDonald say or do then?"

"Well, he said it might make a difference with him if I could tell. Then, he called for a drink, but he didn't get it...for the same reason as before. His credit's no good."

"Anyone with him at this time?"

"Let me see if I can remember.... Yes, it was Melvin Chapman. He was with him."

"Do you remember what day this was?"

Crance shook his head and said he could not remember. He stepped down, and Coroner Bradford called for adjournment until 2 P.M

5

Thomas and Julia Quinlan Testify

Dec. 31, 1894:

Twenty minutes sooner than two o'clock on the last day of 1894 the inquest resumed with Miss Julia Quinlan taking the stand. She looked lovely and unfashionably slender in her Sunday best with her brown hair pulled back into a bun. She confirmed that she was the daughter of the late Patrick Quinlan and agreed to answer questions as best she could.

"What time did your father leave the house on Friday morning, December 21, 1894?"

"He left between 7 and 8 o'clock."

"And when did he return?"

"A few minutes after twelve noon."

"When did he leave the house again?"

"It was a few minutes past 6 o'clock, after he had eaten his supper."

"Did he talk about money with you that day?"

"No, but he gave me my money for the turkeys I raised."

"Did you see him take the money from his pocketbook?"

"No, I just assumed that he had."

"Think carefully for a moment. Had your father recently said anything to indicate that he thought someone was watching him to get his money?"

"No, he never did."

"What did your father do that day between midday and 6 P.M.?"

Julia could not recall. Coroner Bradford paced back and forth momentarily as if lost in thought. Then, he picked up his line of questioning.

"Was it usual for your father to come into the village in the evening?"

Julia replied that he seldom did that.

"Did he say why he was going to the village after he had supper?"

"No."

"Where was your brother when your father left for the village at that time?"

"Tom was in the barn then."

"After your father left, how long was it before your brother returned from the barn?"

Julia said she did not know but she knew he had come in and put some milk for the table in the tub of cold water.

"What time did you retire for the evening?"

"Nine o'clock."

"And your brother?"

"Tom was in the house with me that evening. He retired when I did."

"Was anyone else with the two of you?"

"No, we were alone that evening."

"Do you recall seeing anyone about the premises that day or evening?"

"No, no one."

The coroner then asked her what time she arose the next morning and asked her to describe the series of events of the day.

"I got up Saturday morning at 5:45 A.M. Tom was not up yet. I called him as soon as I had breakfast ready. I told him that Pa was not at home. I told him that Pa must have gone to his brother's or possibly stayed up with Mr. Fanning who was sick in town."

"Was it common for your father to stay away from home nights?"

"No, it was seldom that he did."

"Tell the jury what happened next, please."

"Tom and I went to the barn and milked. Then he started for the milk depot in the village."

"What time was it when he returned?"

"I don't know."

"Please continue."

"He came into the kitchen where I was and said he had found Pa and that both his eyes were black and he looked as though he had got hurt or fallen. He said he had Pa in the wagon and that I had to come and help get him out."

"Was there anything said about your father being intoxicated?"

Julia replied "No," and was quite adamant that she had never seen her father entirely under the influence of liquor.

"Tom and I managed to carry Pa into the house and laid him on his bed. We rubbed him, and we tried to revive him. Tom told me that he found Pa below the bridge and that he had also found some nails, a jackknife, and a plug of tobacco. He said his clothes were on him, except for his hat. We sent for the doctor when our efforts to revive him didn't work. Tom started for the doctor's around a quarter past noon, and he returned soon."

"How soon?

Julia could not remember how soon it was but that Tom told her that Dr. White was busy and would start at 3 P.M. She explained that the doctor arrived and told them that their father could not recover. She struggled to maintain her composure and then continued, "This was the first time that we even supposed Pa was seriously hurt."

Julia gave further testimony which was principally in corroboration with that given by Dr. White. She related the incidents which followed the visit of the priest and doctor. She was able to describe her father's purse but was unable to provide any information concerning her father's papers or private documents. Coroner Bradford thanked her for her testimony.

Julia's brother, Thomas, was next sworn. While Julia had seemed subdued, Thomas started his testimony with an edge.

"Are you the son of the late Patrick Quinlan?"

"I am the son of the murdered Patrick Quinlan."

"Please describe your activities of the morning of December 21st."

"I drove to Homer with a load of poultry at about 10 A.M. I went to the barn of O. B. Andrews. Pa was there already. I returned home at 11:15 A.M. Pa was not there when I arrived. He returned when I was having midday dinner. He gave the money he received for the poultry to Julia, and…."

"Did you actually witness that transaction?" interjected the coroner.

"Well…no…I was eating at the time, but I know…."

Bradford cut in, "Where did your father spend that afternoon?"

"Pa went to the lower pastures and returned a little before 5 o'clock."

"And where were you at this time?" probed the coroner.

Thomas seemed defensive about having to account for his whereabouts.

"Why, I was up at the barns all the time."

34

He went on to state that they all had supper together, at a little after 5 P.M.

"Pa said during supper that he was going to the village after milking. He and I did the milking as usual. Pa got through first. He was just going down the road when I was coming up to the house."

The coroner pushed on, "Did you wake up during the night of December 21, 1894?"

Thomas did not seem comfortable with the questioning but he responded, "No, sir, I slept through the night and did not awake until morning when Julia called me."

"And you started for the milk depot after the cows were milked?"

"Yes, it was a little past 7 A.M."

"Now, as you were driving along, what was the first thing out of the ordinary you noticed?"

"Just after crossin' the bridge I first saw Pa's overcoat on the ground. Then, on closer look, I realized it wasn't just the coat; it was Pa lyiin' by the road, with his face down. And I called to him, but he did not answer."

"And then you drove on to the milk depot?"

"I did."

"What were you thinking, Mr. Quinlan? That was your father lying there."

"As I've said before, I was thinkin' he was drunk," Thomas answered firmly with a touch of anger and frustration in his voice.

"Did you come right back after delivering the milk?" pressed the coroner, looking at the witness over his wire-rimmed glasses.

" I came right back after I stopped at the Domestic Bakery on [No. 6] Main Street."

"I see, and what steps did you take upon returning to your father?"

"When I reached Pa and found him still there, I removed my coat and put it in the back of the wagon. I rolled Pa over and lifted him into the wagon, placed him on the coat, and turned the team and wagon out upon the grass and drove to the house."

"Did you notice at that time that your father's pockets were turned inside out?"

"No, not then, but I saw his jackknife, a plug of tobacco, and some nails on the ground."

"Did you return to this spot later that day?"

"That I did. At about 11 A.M., I went down for a closer look, and I…"

At this point, a stick was thrust toward Thomas, and the coroner asked, "Is this the stick you saw lying near your father when you first discovered him?"

It was not an object Thomas wanted to look at, but he identified it as the stick he had seen near his father. He continued to offer testimony that corroborated the statements made by previous witnesses.

Then, the coroner peered over his spectacles intently at the witness and asked, "Do you admit, Mr. Quinlan, to telling two different stories to the district attorney about when you carried your father back to the house?"

Thomas could not look into the coroner's eyes but, looking down, offered his explanation. "My reason for doin' so was because I was ashamed. I was ashamed of lettin' anyone know of what must seem to be neglect. My reason for leavin' Pa there was I might save time in getting' the milk to the depot and I thought he was drunk and that it would not hurt him to lie a little longer." He paused and then added, "I thought no one would be the wiser if I should."

Thomas was visibly relieved to be excused.

6

Testimony Extends into New Year's Eve

Next to take the stand was Anna Murphy, wife of Michael Murphy, the saloonkeeper at the Homer House who had testified in the morning after John Doyle. She answered the coroner's questions directly but had nothing of substance to add to the case.

Anna was replaced by Patrick O'Conner. O'Conner testified to seeing Patrick Quinlan on the evening of December 21st between six and seven o'clock at Daniel Donahue's restaurant and saloon at 51 South Main in Homer. The coroner asked if others were in the saloon at the same time, and O'Conner gave the names of Charles Healey, Henry Bedell, and some others.

"Did Patrick Quinlan speak with you at that time?"

"That he did."

"What about?"

"He told me how much money he had received that day for turkeys."

"Was he drinking?"

"He drank one glass of ale with me and then left."

"Did you leave with him or follow him?"

"No, he departed and I stayed in Donahue's."

The proprietor of Donahue's, the affable Daniel Donahue, was then called to testify. He confirmed that he, too, had last seen Patrick Quinlan in his pub at 51 South Main between 6:30 and 7 P.M. on the night in question.

"He ordered one glass of ale. Paid five cents for it, and only remained about five minutes."

"Do you recall Louis Clark, John McDonald, or Wilbur Butler being in your establishment on that Friday night?"

"No, none of them were there."

One of the jurors, George A. Eldridge, was summoned to testify next.

"What is your relationship to the deceased, Patrick Quinlan?"

"My farm adjoins the Quinlan farm, and I have known the man ever since he moved to the farm back in 1878."

Eldridge swore that he, too, had seen Quinlan returning home on the Friday evening in question. In giving further statements, Eldridge presented new facts to the jurors. "On the morning after the murder, I found the imprint of a shoe with a pointed toe frozen in the mud in the road opposite to where Patrick was found." This caused some murmuring among those present. "On the Monday after the murder I found part of a post near the barn at the end of the private road. This seems to me, without doubt, to be the post from which the stick found by his body was broken." More murmuring ensued.

Yet another Homer saloonkeeper was then summoned from what seemed to be the village's vast reservoir of drinking establishments. Homer resident, George F. Pratt, keeper of The Inkstand, said he was at his saloon on the 21st of December from early in the afternoon until 11 P.M. and Patrick Quinlan never came in that day. He recalled that Fred Graham, John McDonald, and Lou Clark were in the saloon that day.

"What time did Mr. McDonald come in?"

"I'd say it was about 7 P.M."

"Was he alone?"

"No, Clark was with him."

"Did they order drinks?"

"They asked for drinks, but they got none."

"And why was that?"

"They had no money."

"How long did they stay?"

"About thirty minutes."

Pratt was unable to recall how many times McDonald had been in his pub that day or the hour. He could remember, however, that on one occasion McDonald had spent about one dollar. "He had a two dollar bill on him when he spent a dollar."

A blacksmith in Homer named Fred Graham was next to be questioned. He testified that he boarded at Murphy's Homer House and that he had spent the night of December 21st in his room at Murphy's that he shares with John McDonald.

"Was Mr. McDonald there, too?"

"Yes, sir, John was there, too."

"Anyone else, or just the two of you?"

"There was another man, Lou Clark. He came in with John and spent the night on the couch in the same room."

"Had they been drinking?"

"Yes, a bit too much."

"You mean they were intoxicated?"

"Yes."

Three more men were called -- a carriage painter named John Bennett; a tinsmith named Burt G. Darrow; and another saloonkeeper, Patrick Kinney -- but nothing of importance was gained from their testimonies. By then, an adjournment was taken until 8 P.M.

With only four hours remaining in the year 1894, the inquest entered into an unusual evening session. Nothing substantive was offered by the first three witnesses. Wilbur Arthur Butler threw no light upon the incident of the 21st. Richard F. Randall, Homer resident and owner of a liquor store at 45 South Main, had nothing of interest to add to the case. John O'Connors' testimony was unimportant.

Then George A. McChesney, employee of the Hotel Windsor in Homer [where the Town Hall is now on North Main], gave an account that gained everyone's rapt attention. He claimed that Patrick Quinlan was in the hotel on Friday, December 21, between noon and 1 P.M. Some people listening mentally registered that this was contrary to testimony offered by Julia Quinlan and her brother, Thomas. Hadn't she stated her father had come home around noon, and Thomas said his father had spent the afternoon at the lower pastures? Furthermore, McChesney testified that McDonald had been in the Windsor twice on Tuesday, Christmas Day, both times with Mel Chapman.

"I remember they had a drink the first time between noon and 1 P.M. They both came back again at about 10 P.M. Both were drunk. They asked for drinks on McDonald's credit, but I refused. McDonald started in on me. He argued that he was a 'good man," and then he asked me something bizarre."

"And what was that?" asked the Coroner?

"He asked me if I thought he would kill a man."

40

"And what did you say to that?"

"I told him I thought his statement was a strange one to make on the eve of a murder. He said he was referring to the Quinlan case and that he understood that he was booked for doing the job. Mel Chapman blurted out to McDonald, 'Keep your damned mouth shut!'"

"I see," intoned the Coroner, peering over his glasses intently at the witness, "and did they leave soon after this?"

"No, they sat down in the office and remained there 'til I closed up. And then they refused to leave, they said, until they'd been treated. I refused. I opened the door and told them to get out. McDonald was the first to leave, but Chapman stood in the doorway to prevent the door from closing. He argued awhile but finally let me close the door and lock it. I found it interesting that during their stay they claimed they had a twenty dollar bill, but they never showed it to me."

After that testimony, the statements next made by Charles C. Stone, William G. Berry, George J. Murphy, and George I. Crain were inconsequential. With less than two hours remaining before the arrival of the New Year, Coroner Bradford adjourned the inquest until the following noon.

7

Inquest Verdict Reached on New Year's Day

Jan. 1, 1895:

The New Year dawned in Homer, filled with the promise contained within all things "new." In 27 days, a new electric trolley was scheduled to make an eagerly awaited trial run down Main Street and connect the village with the village of Cortland to the south. The future city of Cortland, the county seat, had already surpassed Homer as the center of commerce. In the village of Homer, the inquest in the Quinlan case resumed at 12:10 PM, giving anyone who may have overindulged the night before some time to recover. Frank Johnson was called first, but he could remember very little and was of no help in the proceedings. Attention now fell upon Louis Clark as he took the stand.

"My name is Louis Clark. I am twenty-five years old. I have lived on King Street in Homer for eleven years."

"What is your occupation?"

"Carriage painter for the Cortland Wagon Company…for the past five weeks anyway."

"You mean you're not employed there now?"

"No, I quit," Clark replied nervously.

"When did you quit?"

"I quit on Friday, December 21st."

This response was followed by a very rigid examination of the former carriage painter, but beyond his testimony that he drank a good many times at a number of different places in Homer on the night of December 21st, little was learned from him. The coroner decided to call a recess for two hours.

Louis Clark took the stand again after the break. He testified that he had first heard of Quinlan's death on the Saturday after the murder.

"But Mr. Quinlan did not succumb until the next day, Sunday," declared the coroner, again peering, in his manner, over his glasses.

"Well, you know what I mean," Clark nervously responded. "Everybody Saturday was saying he'd been struck on the head and wasn't going to make it."

"Did you know Patrick Quinlan?"

"No."

"When he was alive, did you know where he lived?"

"No."

Though questioned further, little of interest was learned from Clark.

Not without anticipation, those in attendance were eager to hear from John McDonald. He was produced next and sworn in, but his testimony was much the same as that just given by Clark. At 8:30 on the evening of the first of January, 1895, John McDonald concluded his testimony, and the evidence presented in the inquest was turned over to the jury. For thirty minutes the jury deliberated. Then foreman Hugh McDermott rendered the verdict: "Patrick Quinlan came to his death on the night of December 21, 1894. Said death was the result of injury received upon the head on December 21st between the hours of 8 o'clock P.M. and 8 o'clock A.M, December 22nd. Said injury was inflicted by a person or persons at present unknown to the jury."

The inquest was dismissed and the jurors discharged by Coroner Bradford at 9 P.M.

Jan. 2, 1895:

It was official; Patrick Quinlan of the Town of Homer, New York, had been murdered, and the murderer was at large. The verdict spread quickly through the village, and those who examined the evidence presented in the day's issue of *The Cortland Evening Standard* regrettably could not find much ground upon which to form a different opinion. The paper reported, "It seems to be the wish of the citizens in this village that the case should not be dropped at this point, but that the county officers should do all in their power to ferret out the perpetrator of this mysterious crime."

Newly elected District Attorney Miles E. Burlingame, having inherited the Quinlan case, came to Homer on Wednesday, January 2, 1895, to speak with several of the jurors from the inquest. He firmly told each of them, "I assure you I will do all in my power to find out and convict the murderer of Patrick Quinlan." The press reported, "If such is the case the new district attorney will do this community a great benefit."

Jan. 7, 1895:

On this date *The Cortland Evening Standard* ran the following blurb on page three:

Reward Offered

The undersigned hereby offer a reward of five
hundred dollars for the apprehension and conviction of the person or persons who murder-
ously assaulted and robbed Patrick Quinlan of
Homer, N.Y., on the night of December 21, 1894.
December 25, 1894
THOMAS QUINLAN
JULIA QUINLAN
860-tf w 597 tf

The next day, the paper ran the same announcement and phone numbers again.

8

Arrests are made in Cortland and Syracuse

April 24, 1895:

Time passed. Winter transitioned to spring. The amount of sunlight per day increased, but no light seemed to be thrown upon the Quinlan murder case. Impatience in Homer with the lack of progress in the past four months was noted in the newspaper on this date: "The people of this village are awaiting the outcome of the proceedings now taking place at the district attorney's office in Cortland...." To say the village was nervous about a murderer being at large was an understatement.

May 4, 1895:

Ten days later, there was movement in the case. Not without protest, John "Jack" McDonald was arrested at his boarding place at 9 Pomeroy Street in Cortland. Sheriff Hilsinger took McDonald into custody just before noon, May 4th. At 2 P.M., the moulder employed by Cortland's Howe Ventilating Stove Company found himself a prisoner standing before Justice of the Peace Dorr C. Smith. McDonald was arraigned on the charge of murder in the first degree of Patrick Quinlan. The prisoner did not plead, and his examination was set down for Friday morning, May 10, at 10 o'clock. District Attorney Burlingame and John Courtney, Jr., appeared for The People, and the Honorable A.P. Smith was assigned as counsel for the defendant. The prisoner was then remanded to the jail to await his examination.

May 4, 1895:

The warrant for McDonald's arrest was not the only warrant issued the night before. The arrest of McDonald was delayed until noon so that there would be no opportunity for the news of his apprehension to reach Syracuse. Armed with a warrant for complicity in the crime, Deputy Sheriff James Edwards had gone to Syracuse to find

Louis Clark, who was believed to be employed in the city as a carriage painter for H. A. Moyer. At 3:30 P.M. of the day of McDonald's arrest, Deputy Edwards telephoned authorities in Cortland that Clark had been arrested by Chief of Detectives Sheppard and Officer Dorner of Syracuse and delivered over to him and Detective Haldebrant of Elmira. They said they would have him brought back to Cortland on the train scheduled to arrive at 6:27 P.M.

"This is the result of a long series of investigations," the public was informed by the *Cortland Evening Standard*. "Deputy Edwards has worked constantly on the case since the murder. Constable Shirley of Homer has also been engaged upon it. Deputy Edwards' theory and his investigations, however, have proved to be the ones which led to these arrests. The facts as they were learned were presented to District Attorney Burlingame and he has left no stone unturned to bring them to a successful issue, and his work was in progress at the very time that he was criticized for inactivity by those who did not know what they were talking about." The *Cortland Democrat* was quick to point out "The fact that they have been arrested does not prove they are guilty and they are entitled to a fair trial."

The public took comfort in knowing that arrests had been made, that twenty-four witnesses had been summoned, three from outside Cortland County, and that the murdered man's pocket book had been found on April 26th in a field on a direct line from the crime scene back to Homer. It was reported that the pocket book had the appearance of having been exposed to the weather for a long time. It was also reported that the law enforcement officers "believe they have the men who committed the murder and believe they have the facts to prove it." The news article concluded with this observation: "If such proves to be the case, it will vindicate the cause of justice in Cortland County which seemed to be slumbering, and much credit will be due to those who were the means of securing the arrests."

An impending criminal trial in Cortland vied for the public's interest in another event scheduled for later in May. Below the news article announcing that McDonald's examination would be on May 10th was the announcement that Sig Sautelle of Homer [the octagon structure on the present Homer-Cortland Road] would be bringing his traveling 10 and 20 cent circus to Cortland on May 16. There would be "several new and novel features" presented "in a single ring which is much more agreeable than the big three ring shows." May promised to be a month filled with anticipation for the curious and those who enjoy a good spectacle.

9

The People vs. John McDonald

May 10, 1895:

For those expecting the trial to get under way in the grand jury room of the courthouse in Cortland [on the site of the present day public library at the corner of Court and Church] on May 10th, there was disappointment. McDonald and Clark entered a plea of not guilty. Attorneys Smith and Dickinson, counsel for defendants McDonald and Clark, moved for separate trials for the defendants and for an adjournment of one week. Justice Dorr C. Smith granted the requests.

Court House, Cortland, N. Y.

May 17, 1895:

In the case of The People vs John McDonald, with District Attorney Burlingame assisting The People, Thomas Dane of 12 Elm Street, Homer, took the witness stand on Friday, May, 17, 1895. A deposition made by him before Justice Smith on May 1st was read to him after which he was cross-examined by Attorney Smith. Dane testified that between 8 and 9 o'clock on the night of December 21, 1894, he was in Doyle's saloon in Homer.

"While I was there, Patrick Quinlan came in through the back way into the barroom. I was in the front room at the time and I heard Quinlan talking about having sold his turkeys on that day. John McDonald and Louis Clark came in from the rear entrance and on through to the front room. I talked with McDonald, and Clark entered into conversation with Albert Salisbury who was in the saloon at the time. McDonald and Clark remained ten or fifteen minutes. Quinlan left the saloon by the rear door, and about five minutes later, McDonald and Clark also left, going out by the front door onto Main Street and heading south. Before they left, I heard Clark say to McDonald 'It's about time for us to go up there.'"

Under cross-examination, Dane admitted that he could not swear positively whether Clark had said "It's about time for us to go" or "It's about time for us to go up there." Dane stated he had been acquainted with Patrick Quinlan for some ten or fifteen years and in that time had never seen him intoxicated. Furthermore, he did not see Quinlan drink anything that night in Doyle's saloon. Dane left Doyle's on the night in question at 9 P.M. and did not see McDonald or Clark after they left the saloon.

Homer farmer Henry D. Keeling was the next witness. He testified to having found a man's pocketbook in his field on the Friday preceding the first of May.

"I found it about one hundred rods from where Quinlan was found hurt and about one rod [16.5 feet] from the highway. It had the appearance of having lain on the ground for some time. Later, it was identified as belonging to Patrick Quinlan."

The DA showed a pocketbook to the witness.

"Yes, that is the one I found," Keeling affirmed.

"And where did you find it?"

"I found it on a steep side hill and in the most direct line from where Quinlan was found to Homer Village, after turning aside to avoid a barbed wire fence."

"How long have you known the late Patrick Quinlan?"

Keeling could not answer the question precisely but said he had known Quinlan "for a number of years." He confirmed that he had often seen him passing across his farm when going on foot from his home to Homer or when returning from Homer. He added, "He did not usually go within twenty rods of where I found his pocketbook."

A nineteen year resident of nearby Ithaca, New York, Ann Oatman was then called to the stand. The DA, pointing in the direction of the defendant, asked her to identify him. She said he was John or "Jack" McDonald. Her testimony was as follows:

"A detective from Elmira, named Hildebrand, came to my house last October and then again around the first of May. He was the first man I ever told about McDonald comin' to my house. I first met "Jack" three or four years ago. He was at my house last winter. He had come from Cortland. He said the coroner's jury was a pack of fools. I did not know then, from what he was sayin', that anyone had been killed. He said 'Everything is dark against me' and that he was goin' to Trumansburg to see his mother. I could tell he'd been adrinkin'. He asked for somethin' to eat. He said he was lookin' for work. He also said that he had somethin' in his breast pocket he could use and that he had used it on former occasions. A short time afterward I saw him at the Reeves house in Ithaca. I told him, 'In my opinion, honesty is the best policy.'"

The defense picked up on this line and made a direct stab at discrediting the truthfulness of the witness during cross-examination.

"Ann Oatman. That's not your real name, is it?"

"No. My real name is Ann Straight," the witness responded matter-of-factly. Eyebrows raised in the courtroom.

"And your maiden name?"

"Johnson. My father's name was Johnson."

"Is it not true that you are coming forth to testify now against the defendant because you know there is a reward offered for the apprehension and conviction of the murderer of Mr. Quinlan?"

The witness shook her head and adamantly denied any knowledge of any reward.

After the woman of many names, the next to be called was a woman named Amelia Reeves. She testified that she lived in Ithaca and that McDonald had, indeed, been at her house last January.

Called next to testify was John Doyle. He confirmed that he kept a saloon in Homer, knew Patrick Quinlan, and remembered the night of the murder.

"McDonald and Clark were in my saloon that night. Soon after 8 o'clock Patrick remarked that it was time he was goin' home, and after drinkin' a glass of beer, he went out at the back door. He wasn't drunk, and I never seen him drunk but once…and that was two or three years ago."

"Who came into the saloon first, Quinlan or McDonald and Clark?" probed the attorney.

"Patrick came in first that night by the back door. McDonald and Clark followed about two minutes later. Albert Saulsbury bought drinks for McDonald and Clark. Then they went into the front room and sat down on a window sill eight or ten feet from where Patrick was sittin' at a table."

"Were McDonald and Clark intoxicated?"

"They had been drinkin' but they were not drunk, if that's what you mean."

"Was there any conversation between Mr. Quinlan and the other two men?"

"I don't recall any talk. I didn't hear any conversation between 'em."

"Did you have any conversation with McDonald or Clark?"

"No, I did not."

"Did you hear either of the two men say anything before Mr. Quinlan left the saloon?"

"Yes. Clark said to McDonald, 'If we are goin' up there we had better go,' and then they went out the front door after Patrick had left."

"Do you know which way they went after leaving your place?"

"No," Doyle responded with a shake of his head. He finished by confirming that he had given sworn testimony at the inquest before Coroner Bradford and had had no conversation with the defendant on the subject since the assault upon Quinlan.

10

Reputable and Disreputable Witnesses

May 17, 1895:

Occupying the witness stand next was the respected coroner, Dr. George D. Bradford. Peering over his wire rimmed glasses in his customary manner, he related for the Court how he had examined the body of Patrick Quinlan on Monday, December 24, 1894.

"I found an injury about two inches above and in front of the right ear. The skull was broken into small pieces at this place, and the pieces of bone were driven into the lining of the brain. These pieces had been removed surgically before I examined the body."

"In your professional opinion, what was the immediate cause of death?"

"Death was brought on by the pressure of blood clot on the brain. There were two blood clots -- one just above the wound and the other at the base of the brain eight or nine inches from the first. Three lines of fracture radiated from the wound. One line ran from the wound to the base of the brain, eight or nine inches from the wound."

"Did you find any other injuries?"

"On the back of the head, the scalp was bruised, and there was a settling of blood underneath it. This and the opening made to remove the pieces of bone from the wound were the only pathologies noticed."

"So the brain clearly showed evidence of sustaining an impact resulting in fatality?"

"Yes, the entire brain substance was much congested."

"In addition to the brain, were other bodily organs damaged?"

"Just the brain. The other internal organs were in a normal condition."

"In your opinion, would a club of large size produce the effect to the head and brain you described, Doctor?"

"Yes, it could...if used with sufficient force."

"Do you think a man could be conscious after receiving a blow struck with sufficient force to produce the wounds you examined?"

"No, a man could not remain conscious after such a blow."

"From your examination of the body, how many blows had been struck?"

"Two...two blows were struck."

"In your professional opinion, could the blows have been received by the man falling?"

"No, we can rule out the injuries being caused by the man merely falling."

Following through with medical testimony, Dr. White of Homer next recalled being called to see Patrick Quinlan on the day before he died. He stated that he arrived there around 8 P.M. and found Quinlan on a bed breathing heavily and unconscious.

"I found blood in his mouth and nose. His tongue was swollen...about twice its normal size. His hands were covered with blood, but I found no wounds on them. There was a contused wound on the front side of his head above the right ear."

The doctor affirmed that Quinlan never regained consciousness and that on the next night, Sunday, he, Dr. Higgins, and Dr. Robinson removed pieces of bone from the wound.

"And did Mr. Quinlan die about one half hour after that procedure was performed?"

"Yes, he did."

"And is it your opinion that Mr. Quinlan died from a compression of the brain produced by injuries inflicted upon his head by some object in the hands of some person other than Mr. Quinlan himself?"

"That is my opinion, yes."

With the prosecution making a solid case for the commitment of a murder, the examination was adjourned to 9 o'clock Saturday morning.

May 18, 1895:

Upon resumption of the criminal trial on Saturday, May 18, 1895, Fred Graham took the stand for questioning.

"Did you know Patrick Quinlan?"

"I did."

"Do you remember your whereabouts the night of Mr. Quinlan's murder?"

"I do."

"Can you point out for the Court one John or "Jack" McDonald?"

The witness pointed toward the defendant sitting at a table.

"Can you tell us where the defendant, John McDonald, was living at the time of the murder?"

"Sure. Jack was boarding at Michael Murphy's in Homer in the same room as me for three or four weeks or until December 31st. Actually, I guess it was about ten days after that date that he left, and I stayed there for another three weeks."

Graham described how he knew McDonald had gone from Murphy's to The Inkstand on the Monday morning after the injury to Quinlan.

"You see," Graham recounted with a smile, "Jack tried to climb over a wire fence behind the school on the Green. Got all tangled up and managed to cut his hand and legs in the process. He was quite the sight."

Graham was next asked to recall the whereabouts of the defendant on the night of December 21st.

"I'd been out huntin' on that Friday. And when I returned to my room at the hotel, I went to bed. That was 8 P.M. Jack and Lou Clark came in about 10 P.M. Lou had taken sick and laid down on the couch. I told Jack not to let Lou do any vomitin' on the carpet. Jack and I stepped out of doors for five minutes. When we returned, Jack retired. I think Clark had passed out on the couch; they were pretty drunk, you know, when they came in."

"Did you ever see Patrick Quinlan drunk?"

"Never saw Patrick drunk but once, I'd say."

"What was the usual time Mr. McDonald went to bed nights?"

Graham could not recall the exact time of McDonald's retiring on any night.

"I know I did not hear the town clock [Congregational Church clock] strike 10 or 11 any night he went to bed during the four weeks we roomed together. And on any night in that time I was usually in bed by 7 o'clock. Had to get up one night in his presence to nail the door to the room shut. The cold weather was beginnin' to come in."

Graham then was asked to step down, and Thomas Gerrard took the stand. Gerrard knew Patrick Quinlan and had known John McDonald since 1885. He was asked to oblige the Court by recalling an event that had happened after the murder of Patrick Quinlan.

"Well, I saw McDonald in a saloon on Port Watson Street in Cortland, one night. A woman, Cora Godfrey, was there in the sitting room. She was with a man. She and McDonald got into a bit of an altercation. And in the course of it she blurted out to McDonald 'You remember the Quinlan case.' McDonald told her, 'You keep still.' He and I then went out in the street, and I said to him 'She gave you a bad blast in there.' And he replied that if she didn't keep still it would make him trouble."

The defense attorney then cross-examined, knowing the prosecution was trying to show that the defendant was inclined to keep company with an unsavory crowd.

"Isn't it true you have been going around in recent weeks asking several people about the Quinlan case?"

"So?" blurted back Gerrard.

"Isn't it also true that you have been paid money to find the perpetrators of the crime in the Quinlan case?"

"No, that's a lie," responded Gerrard angrily.

The Defense pushed on. "Isn't it true you have received money or the offer of money from Constable Shirley of Homer to locate the culprits?"

"Sir, I have been given no money nor the offer of money by Constable Shirley or any other person to get the murderers."

"Oh, no? What about the money Dennis Quinlan offered you? What was that for?"

Gerrard furrowed his brow and showed a reticence to answer. He glanced toward Justice Smith, who instructed him to answer the question.

With lowered eyes and lowered voice, the witness reluctantly replied, "Dennis Quinlan offered me money to get McDonald drunk."

"Why was that?"

"To pick his pocket," responded the witness in a nearly inaudible voice.

"And did you do it?" pressed the defense.

"No, I never tried to get him drunk," answered Gerrard quite clearly now, "but I told him what had been said about it and what Quinlan was trying to get me to do."

"When did this take place?"

"About three weeks after the murder."

"Is it true that you worked in the same shop with Mr. McDonald for some time after the murder?"

"Yes."

"For how long?"

"For some five or six weeks."

"In the same shop?"

"Yes."

"And in that time, did Mr. McDonald ever act like a person trying to escape from an uncomfortable situation?"

"No, he did not."

The defense seemed satisfied with the affirmation given of his client's upstanding character and continued on.

"One last question. Now think carefully. Constable Shirley did pay you money to track down the perpetrators of the murder, isn't that so?"

"Shirley gave me two cents to take the electric trolley to Cortland."

"And that was for what purpose?" probed the attorney.

"To find out where Louis Clark was," replied Gerrard.

By late morning, Thomas Quinlan, son of the man murdered in the winter solstice, was summoned to the stand. Once again, he testified to his father's selling of some turkeys in Homer and receiving about $40 for them on December 21, 1894. He recounted his father's return to Homer on the same day at 6 in the evening. He said he saw nothing of his father until the next morning when going to the milk depot, and then he found him lying by the side of the road with his face in his hands.

"I thought Pa was asleep. He seemed to be snoring."

"Did you try to rouse him?"

"I called out to him. He didn't answer."

"Did you tend to him right then?"

"No. I didn't get out o' the wagon. I continued on to Homer, delivered the milk, came back, and lifted Pa into the wagon. I took him home, and with my sister's help, carried him into the house."

"Now, you summoned a physician that afternoon for your father. Why didn't you think to act sooner?"

"I don't know…I never saw a person unconscious before. I thought he was sleepin' off a hangover."

"Did you detect the odor of liquor on your father's breath?"

"No, there was no smell of liquor."

Attorney Smith approached the witness to cross-examine.

"Mr. Quinlan, when you first saw your father Saturday morning in his unfortunate state, what did you think had happened?"

"I thought he had been out with the boys the night before and was probably drunk."

"I see. And was your father accustomed to doing this…to remain away all night 'with the boys,' as you say?"

"No."

"But you would admit that sometimes he did?"

"Yes."

"And when you came upon your father, you did not think he had lain on the ground all night?"

"I had no reason to suspect that."

"And you felt no compunction to get off the wagon to rouse your father?"

"I was in a hurry to deliver the milk before it could go bad."

60

"And yet you told some people that you turned around immediately and took your father home before going on with the milk. Why two different stories, Mr. Quinlan?"

"I was concerned what people would think…that they would think I was neglectful of Pa."

Since a mid-day meal was not to be neglected, Justice Smith called for adjournment until 1:30 P.M., and Thomas Quinlan seemed much relieved.

11

Conflicting Testimony of Thomas Quinlan

May 18, 1895:

Thomas Quinlan's relief was of short duration. In what seemed like no time at all he was back on the stand for what would be a full afternoon of questioning and cross-examination.

"You testified this morning, Mr. Quinlan, that you told two different accounts of your actions after finding your father in the road. Can you explain to the court what motivated you to tell two different stories?"

"I had learned from the Syracuse newspapers that suspicion rested on me. Actually, I had not seen the articles in the newspapers but, rather, I had heard people talkin' about them. So when I went before the district attorney it was with the knowledge that I was the suspected party, and…."

The defense attorney interrupted, "Who suggested to you to change the story about turning around and taking your father home before going on with the milk."

"No one. No one did," shot back Thomas with a scowl.

"So, if we are to believe the story that you went on with the milk, why should we not see you as neglectful of your father as he is left outside on a winter's day?"

Thomas took on a defensive tone, as if he were the defendant in this murder trial.

"Listen, it was not a chilly morning. I even started out with an overcoat, but I took it off when returnin' from the milk station."

"What time did you reach the milk station?"

"Around 8 A.M."

"And after unloading the milk you did not hurry back to your father but went next to the bakery on six South Main Street. Is that correct?"

"Yes, that's what I did."

"And what thoughts of your father did you have at that time?"

"Why....I supposed he was lying on the ground at this time."

"While you were purchasing some goods of Miss Johnston at the bakery?"

"We needed bread back home," snapped Thomas.

"All right. So you say you took the milk to the depot, went to the Johnston sisters' bakery on Main Street, and started for home. When you came upon your father, was he in about the same position as when you say you first saw him?

"He was in the same position, about eight feet from the wagon track. I noticed then that his trousers were open and the common leather belt he wore was unbuckled, one end partly under him and the other to one side."

"Did you make an effort to wake him up then?"

"I did. After getting his foot out from under the fence, I took hold of him by his shoulders and told him to 'wake up' or 'brace up'. He did not wake up."

"Go on. And then what?"

"I took hold of him under his arms and pulled him up to the road and got him in the wagon as best I could alone. I took my own overcoat and a heavy woolen ulster which was on the wagon seat and put it under Pa's head and drove home."

"You must have seen tracks on the ground in the area around where you found your father."

"No, I didn't notice any."

"Why was that?"

"Because I wasn't lookin' for tracks, under the circumstance." Thomas was put out by the line of questioning.

"How did you know your father was still alive when you were pulling him toward the wagon?"

"He was snorin'….or what I took for snorin'."

"What time was it when you reached home with your father?"

"Around nine in the morning."

"And when you and your sister carried your father into the house, did your father show any signs of consciousness or physical strength?"

"No. None."

"Was his clothing torn?"

"No, it didn't seem to be."

"From nine o'clock on, what did you do that day?"

"From nine to eleven o'clock I was doin' chores, as usual, feedin' and takin' care of the cows and horses. Around 11 o'clock, I went down, on foot, to where I had found Pa."

"Why did you go back?"

"To look for Pa's pocketbook."

"Did you find it?"

"No, but in lookin' around, that's when I found the track of a small shoe in the road. Size 7, I thought, facing down the hill toward the village."

"This track you say you found was in snow or mud or what?"

"It was in soft mud; it wasn't frozen at the time."

"This was the only track marks you noticed?"

"Other than Pa's two tracks facing almost directly west toward the house. The single track was farther down the hill than Pa's. It looked as though a person had been walkin' on the strip of grass in the center of the road and one foot had slipped off, makin' the track."

"Was this the track mark of a pointed shoe?"

"I can't say that I recall."

"How far from the spot where you found your father did you go in search of his pocketbook that day?"

"Twenty rods."

"And nothing else unusual was found there, correct?"

"The mud in the road there seemed to be flattened down…as if by treading."

"What time did you go back home?"

"About 11:30."

"And your father was still unconscious?"

"Yes, he was still unconscious. Even though I shook him and spoke to him, he did not answer."

"And you say you did not detect the odor of liquor about him, correct?"

"That's right."

"Yet you maintain you still thought he had been drinking?"

"Yes, that's what I thought."

"At what time did you first think something more serious was wrong with your father?"

"It was about twelve noon, and as Pa still showed no signs of comin' to, I began to think something was strange about his condition. A half hour later, I headed out for the village to get Dr. White."

"Dr. White is your family physician?"

"No, we have no family physician, but I had been to see him once before for myself."

"What time did you arrive in Homer?"

"I'm not sure. It may have been 1:30....or maybe closer to 2."

"Really? It took you over one hour to reach Homer?

Thomas shifted nervously in the chair and then answered, "Well...on the way I stopped at the lower place and let out the cows."

"And that took you how long?"

"I was there about ten minutes, I'd say."

"At Dr. White's...can you recall the conversation you had with him?"

"I described Pa's condition for him, and he asked if Pa was in the habit of getting full. I said he was not. He said that Pa must have had a shock or been waylaid and that I had better go out and make inquiries as to whether he had been drinking liquor. He said he would come along as soon as his office hours were done."

"And then you left?"

"Yes. Dr. White said he was expecting a patient. So I left."

"You then came immediately home?"

"No. I visited somel of the saloons in town first and then started for home."

"You stopped in the saloons for drinks?"

"No, of course not," said Thomas with another scowl. "I stopped in, as Doc White had said I should, to ask if Pa had been drinkin' in town the night before."

The attorney pressed on. "Did you make any other stops, besides the saloons, before reaching home?"

"I stopped again at the lower place to put up the cattle."

"And that took you how long?"

"Between an hour and an hour and a half."

"So you reached home at what time?"

"Four or 4:30 P.M."

"And Dr. White arrived when?"

"Soon after I did."

"Did you see the doctor examine your father?"

"I did."

"What did he tell you?"

"He said there was a pressure on Pa's brain, that he had been waylaid and clubbed, and that there wasn't much hope of his recovery."

"What did you do next?"

"I told Dr. White to notify the proper authorities. And then I went to the village that night and came on to Cortland to fetch Father John McLoughlin. Father John returned with me, and then I brought him back to Cortland."

VERY REV. JOHN J. McLOGHLIN, Pastor St. Mary's Catholic Church.

7

"Did you come directly back home?" The barrage of questions continued.

"No, I stopped at a drug store and got some arnica and brandy which Father John said I should get for Pa."

"What time was it when you reached home again?"

"Just before midnight."

"Had there been any change in your father's condition?"

"No, he was in about the same condition as before."

"When did the sheriff and district attorney arrive?"

"They both came on Sunday and again on the next day."

"Now, you offered a reward of $500 for the capture of the perpetrators of the murder. Is that correct?"

"'Tis."

"Was that your idea?"

"The district attorney made the suggestion Monday that I should offer a reward. I did not decide to do so right then but told Mr. Burlingame that I and my sister would come to his office in Cortland that evening and talk it over."

"Did the two of you call at his office that evening?"

"No, we did not go to Cortland that evening. Instead, I went alone Tuesday morning, and Mr. Burlingame drew up a form, which I signed and took home for Julia to sign. I then mailed it out."

"You testified earlier that you heard it had been reported in the papers that your father had been killed and that you were suspected of having committed the crime. Was this before or after you went to the district attorney?"

"It was before."

The defense attorney paced back and forth as if trying to think where to go next with his questioning. He stopped, looked intently at the witness, and asked, "What does the name Hildebrandt mean to you?"

"He's a detective, or calls himself one."

"Is it not true that you have hired this so-called detective to work on the case?"

"No, that is not true." The scowl returned.

"Then, what is your relationship to Mr. Hildebrandt?"

"I did not seek out Mr. Hildebrandt. I had never heard of him 'til a couple weeks after Pa's death. That's when Julia received a letter from him. Hildebrandt came to our place with Sheriff Hilsinger, and he took the letter with him."

"So you never requested Hildebrandt enter the case nor offer him compensation?"

Thomas raised his voice: "I want the record to show that I never asked Hildebrandt to take on the case. I never offered to pay him, and I have not authorized anyone else, for that matter, to compensate him for his time, trouble, or expenses. He probably saw the reward posted in the paper."

Thomas was asked when the notice of the reward was published. He responded that he thought it was about December 26 or 27, but it actually ran on January 7 and 8, almost three weeks after the murder.

"No one as yet has claimed the reward," he testified.

12

Finances on the Farm

May 18, 1895:

The defense next shifted the focus of the questioning to the property of the Quinlan Farm.

"Did your father, Patrick Quinlan, own the farm located on Lots 33 and 34 in the Town of Homer?"

Thomas answered, "When mother died she left me and Julia mortgages of $1,000 each against the farm. In the seventeen years since, no payment has been made."

"You mean your father was supposed to be paying off the mortgage held by you and your sister?"

"Yes."

"And how much, combining the principal and interest, would you say is now due?"

"About $6,000…but not a dollar of it has been asked for by us."

"Nor paid by your late father. Is that so?"

"'Tis."

"So the indebtedness has stood for the past seventeen years?"

"Yes, it has. But we said nothing about it."

"Did your mother leave a will at her passing?"

"She did, but we never went to the trouble of having it proved."

"So three of you -- your father, your sister, and you -- have been living together on the farm since your mother died. Is that so?"

"'Tis."

"So what was the financial understanding among the three of you?"

"Julia received the poultry money…from the chickens and turkeys she raised. I got money from Pa whenever I asked for it."

"Did you get money *whenever* you asked for it? Were you ever denied?"

"Whenever I asked, I always got it." Thomas' response was quite firm.

"Did you keep a book account between you?"

"No, we kept no ledger."

"The farm was in your father's name, except for the mortgage?"

"Yes."

"Were you comfortable with this arrangement?"

"About a year ago Pa wanted me to take the farm and run it by myself and assume all the responsibilities, but I said to Pa 'You'd better go ahead with it; your head is better than mine.'"

"Did your father have any enemies, as far as you know?"

"Pa never had an enemy that I knew of."

"And how did he treat you?"

Thomas appeared to bristle at the question but kept his composure and answered directly, "Pa always treated me kindly and pleasantly. He was a man of amiable disposition with everyone."

"Now you and your sister occupied rooms upstairs at your home and your father slept downstairs. Is that so?"

"'Tis."

"And whenever your father went out evenings, the door was left unlocked for him. Is that so?"

"'Tis."

"Mr. Quinlan, do you know Deputy Sheriff Shirley of Homer?"

"I do."

"Would you say he has taken an active part in trying to find your father's murderer?"

"Yes, he has."

"And the incentive was the $25 you paid him. Correct?"

Thomas registered surprise that McDonald's attorney knew about the money.

"When did you give him the $25?" the attorney probed.

"About a month ago."

"Thank you, Mr. Quinlan. No more questions for today." The attorney turned to the judge and stated, "Your honor, the defense desires to ask a few questions of a witness from Buffalo next, that he might not be compelled to return here again Monday."

Justice Smith excused Thomas Quinlan until Monday, and Elbert Salisbury took the stand. Salisbury said that last December he worked in McGrawville but his home was in Homer. He said he was in John Doyle's saloon on December 21, 1894, at a little after 7 o'clock.

"Quite a number were there: Thomas Davis, Alex Stewart, John Doyle, and others. I went in and took a glass of beer. Louis Clark and John McDonald came in the back door. I bought them a drink, drank again myself, and then went into the sitting room to talk with Davis. Clark and McDonald joined us and talked with Davis and me. I was only there for two or three minutes and then went out."

"Did Clark and McDonald leave with you?"

"No, they were still there when I left."

"Did you know Patrick Quinlan?"

"Only by sight."

"Did you see Patrick Quinlan in Doyle's that evening?"

"No, sir, I did not."

"Was there anyone drinking at Doyle's that you did not know?"

"Someone else was at the bar, but I did not know who he was."

The district attorney wished to cross-examine Salisbury about his character and previous contacts with Louis Clark. He managed to extract from him the recollection of going one night to Charles Rowe's with Clark.

"Now, Charlie Rowe's place is the Park Hotel on Homer Avenue [now the site of Fabio's Restaurant], isn't that so?"

Salisbury indicated that that was so.

"How long ago was this, Mr. Salisbury?" asked the DA.

"It must have been at least two years ago," answered the witness.

"What time of night was it?"

"We got there from Homer at about midnight or closer to 1 A.M.. I'm not sure."

Salisbury began to fidget.

"You were there for what purpose?"

The witness wished he were somewhere else at that moment. He answered, "We took a room for the rest of the night."

"And there were women present?"

"No, we didn't see any women there."

"I see," uttered the lawyer. He made no effort to hold back a smile.

"We went to the place there but we didn't know how tough a reputation it had," a red-faced Salisbury told the court. The lawyer was satisfied with the response and continued to grin sardonically.

"Thank you, Mr. Salisbury. That will do."

Salisbury was excused at 5:10 P.M., and the examination was adjourned until Monday.

May 20, 1895:

Monday, May 20, 1895, rolled around, and Thomas Quinlan was summoned again to the stand, but he did not appear. In his absence, Sheriff Adam Hilsinger was called. He confirmed that he had arrested John, called "Jack," McDonald in Cortland on May 4, 1895, on the charge of murder in the first degree in causing the death of Patrick Quinlan on the night of December 21, 1894. District Attorney Burlingame produced a letter, handed it to the sheriff, and asked him to identify what it was.

"This is a letter I found in McDonald's pocket that I thought might have some bearing on the case. It is addressed to John McDonald of Trumansburg, New York. It's dated January 24, 1895, from Miss Josie Corl of Homer, Cortland County, New York."

"Please read it aloud for the court, Sheriff Hilsinger," requested Burlingame.

The witness obliged, though he stumbled over portions because it was not written in the best English and showed no mastery of punctuation.

"Dear Mark, received your letter today and hasten to answer it. I am not very happy tonite have bin sick all day. But am better since I got your letter you ask me if Fred Graham is in Homer he is not he is in Cortland now Dear they had him and Lue Clark and Mick sworn again last Saturday Mick said Clark was scared to death he told me all about it I wish you could no what the fool sed. Good by my Dear boy I am your ever true friend. Miss Josie Corl."

Upon the arrival in the courtroom of Thomas Quinlan, his name was called, and he returned to the stand. The district attorney wanted to clarify a few points. First was the matter of money in the Quinlan family.

"Is it true, Mr. Quinlan, that you received from your father a salary for your work done on the farm?"

"'Tis. I had an agreement with Pa the year I turned 21 whereby I was to receive a salary for my work."

"And that agreement was honored?"

"Yes."

"How much money did you receive each year?"

"I really can't say…I have no way of knowing how much Pa paid me from year to year."

"Well can you give an approximation for the past two years?'

"I figure I received in bulk $100 last year…and $150 the year before."

Next, the district attorney wanted to focus again on the crime scene.

"Please describe the club you found near your father's body on the day after the assault."

"The club looked as though it had been freshly broken off from smithing, and one nail in the club showed a fresh break."

"Was there blood on the club?"

"I didn't notice any blood on the club."

"Is there a reason your father might not have been aware of persons walking up behind him?"

"Yes. Pa was hard of hearing and probably would not have heard anyone approaching him from behind."

"And you heard no strange sounds in the night, or your father calling out for help?"

"No, I heard nothing, and I don't think a voice could be heard from the place where I found him to the house."

"From the time your father left the house for Homer, you never saw him again until when?"

"The first I saw of Pa was Saturday morning when the horses shied out of the road when they came up near his body."

"Now, is it true that one reason you did not turn the lumber wagon around that morning was because you felt you could not do so very well at that place?"

"It would have been difficult. The road is narrow and there's a shallow ditch on each side."

"And you felt that it was warm enough to leave him lying there until your return from Homer?"

"I did."

"Can you tell the court how your father was dressed that morning?"

"Pa had on a pair of drawers, two pair of overalls, and a pair of wool pants...and an overcoat."

"In which pocket did your father usually carry his pocketbook, knife, or tobacco?"

"I have no idea."

The district attorney then leaned in a little closer to the witness, as one might do when about to share a confidence, and said, "I would like to ask you, Mr. Quinlan...Has there ever been any trouble or hard words between you and your father concerning either you or your sister getting married? Did that topic come up as a source of contention?"

"Never," adamantly responded Thomas, "Never."

"Since the death of your father, with the exception of Deputy Sheriff Shirley and the offer of a $500 reward, have you employed, paid, or offered to pay any attorney or officers of the law?"

"No, I have not."

"And since the death of your father have you counseled with attorneys other than me and the former District Attorney, Mr. Squires?"

"No, I have not."

A certain tiredness and tension was discernible in the verbal exchange.

13

The Crime Scene and an Injured Hand

May 20, 1895:

After a break, Thomas Quinlan, son of the murdered Patrick Quinlan of Homer, again took the stand on the afternoon of May 20, 1895. The district attorney opened by asking how many times he had returned to the crime scene since his father's death.

Thomas responded, "Only twice. Last Saturday, on the way home from Homer, I went on the road, with the purpose of seein' the pocketbook which I had been told Mr. Keeling's son Fred had found while plowin' and which was believed to be Pa's. I saw Mr. and Mrs. Keeling and Mr. Keeling's brother but I was told that Fred had the pocketbook and that he was in Homer. So, I drove home. The next day, Sunday, the pocketbook was sent over to me. That time and the first time I was summoned as a witness before Justice Smith were the only times I've driven around by that road since Pa's death."

Thomas was also asked if he had ever had to assist his father into the house when he had been under the influence of liquor. Thomas recalled that he had done so only on two or three different occasions.

The prosecution next called George W. Eldridge, forty-one year old farmer, who had known Patrick Quinlan as his neighbor since 1878. Their farms adjoined each other. He testified that he had seen and talked with Thomas Quinlan on the morning of Saturday, December 22, but Thomas had mentioned nothing about his father's misfortune. After hearing of the murder on Sunday, December 23, Eldridge said he, out of great curiosity, had gone up to the place where the body had been found.

"I saw blood on the ground," he told the court.

"Was that all?" asked the district attorney.

"No, sir. I came across the track of a pointed shoe or boot in the mud."

"What size shoe or boot do you think it was?

"The size was about eight or nine, I think."

"Pointing in what direction?"

"Northeast."

"And did you come across anything on the ground that could have been used to bludgeon a man?"

Eldridge reflected for a moment and then said, "I don't recall anything. The ground was quite stony, but I don't remember if there was a stone of suitable size to strike a man down with."

"Now, Mr. Quinlan's pocketbook. Is it true that it was found on a direct line, cross lots, toward the village from where the body was found?"

"Yes, sir, 'tis so."

The prosecution pushed on. "Is it your opinion that beyond where the pocketbook was found one could avoid the barbed wire fences by going through the bars that lead to the dugway and then to the Scott Road?"

"Yes."

"Is it also true that you saw a club in the road and thought you could find where it came from?"

"Well, I didn't find the club that was said to be in the road. Later on, I found on the west side of the barway a post that had been broken off. It was a fresh break, and I learned later that the two pieces fitted well together. I understand that boards had been nailed to them; both pieces had nails or parts of nails in them."

"In your judgment," probed the prosecution, "would it have been possible for a lumber wagon to turn around in the road near where the body was found?"

"Possible, but difficult. Not without picking up and carrying one end of the wagon," answered Eldridge.

"Did Patrick Quinlan have a reputation for excessive drinking?"

"No."

"Did you ever see him drunk?"

"Only about a year ago…and maybe once before that. That's all."

"Did Patrick Quinlan have a reputation for quarreling?"

"No. I have never known him to quarrel with anyone."

"How about with members of his own family?"

"In all the years we have been neighbors I did not know of any trouble or hard feeling between any members of the Quinlan family."

"Just one final question for you, Mr. Eldridge. If you had come across a drunken man with an overcoat on, lying on the ground on the morning of December 22nd, would you have been inclined to leave him?"

"I guess…I guess I would not have thought he would suffer by lying there a little while longer."

"That is all, your honor."

The witness was excused at 4:45 P.M., and Justice Smith declared, "On account of the special term of court to convene at the court house Tuesday morning, this examination will adjourn until Friday morning, May 31, at 10 o'clock, at which time all witnesses not yet sworn will be expected to appear." And the gavel came down.

THE GREEN, HOMER, N Y.

May 31, 1895:

Justice Smith brought the gavel down again at forty-five minutes after 10 A.M. on May 31, and proceedings resumed with the forty-four year old proprietor of The Inkstand, George F. Pratt, taking the stand. Pratt acknowledged making depositions of April 26 and May 3 and, upon questioning, offered new information.

"When did you first hear of the murder?"

"In the forenoon of the Saturday after the crime had been committed."

"How long have you known Patrick Quinlan?"

"About twenty-five years."

"On the night of the murder, was Patrick Quinlan in The Inkstand?"

"He was."

"Do you recall the time he left the saloon?"

"Yes, he was there until about 10 or 11 o'clock."

In cross-examination it came out that Pratt's recollection was none too reliable, since he had testified at the inquest that Patrick Quinlan had never darkened his door on December 21st.

"Was the defendant in your saloon that evening?"

"He was there sometime between six and seven o'clock, I think. That's the best I can recall."

"Was he alone?"

"No, Louis Clark was with him."

"Were they in the saloon later that night?"

"I can't recall. I don't think they were."

"When was the next time you saw John McDonald?"

"I saw him the next day, Saturday."

"At what time?"

"I'm not sure of the time….maybe it was 8 or 9 o'clock in the morning."

"But you are certain of the date…Saturday, December 23rd?"

"Oh, it was Saturday all right. Because I remember Fred Graham came in to my place just before McDonald entered. Fred was laughing. He said McDonald had got himself caught on a fence and couldn't get unstuck. He said McDonald was coming from the opposite direction from the school ground when he tangled with the fence, and the fence won. Then, McDonald came in and I saw that his hand was bleeding…near the fleshy part of the thumb. I got a cloth and did up his hand as best I could."

"Did you hear the testimony made earlier by Mr. Fred Graham?"

"Yes, I heard it."

"And do you agree with Mr. Graham that the defendant could just as easily have gone through an opening in the screen wire fence behind the Academy that was a mere two or three rods further along from where the defendant claimed to have gotten stuck on the top wire of the fence -- a wire that was the only barbed wire on a five foot high fence?"

"If you mean do I think McDonald could have gone through the opening like Fred Graham said he did…yes, I do."

Saloonkeeper Pratt was followed on the stand by forty-one year old saloonkeeper Patrick Kinney. Kinney acknowledged his deposition of April 24th and said he had known Patrick Quinlan since they were young boys. He testified that Patrick Quinlan was not in his saloon the evening before the murder but McDonald and Clark were.

"The two men were there at what time?"

"Seven or eight o'clock, I think."

"When they left, did they say where they were going next?"

"I did not hear 'em say where they were goin', but I later was told they went to The Inkstand."

82

"Was Mr. McDonald under the influence of liquor when you saw him?"

"McDonald was."

"And Mr. Clark was, too?"

"I cannot say that Clark was, but McDonald was."

"Can you tell us anything about Mr. McDonald's injured hand?"

Kinney responded that he did not know anything about that.

At this point, the defense decided to recall saloonkeeper George Pratt, and they managed to extract from him a statement to the effect that he thought he refused drinks to McDonald and Clark on the evening of December 21st.

All eyes turned next upon Miss Julia Quinlan as she took the stand to offer testimony.

14

Curious Testimony of Julia Quinlan

May 31, 1895:

Julia Quinlan, upon the stand, gave her age, 34, and stated she had resided in the Town of Homer all her life since seven months old. The account she gave of the circumstances concerning the return of her father to the house the morning after the injury, when he was brought up by his son, was substantially the same as her brother's. She admitted that her father had come home intoxicated before the date in question and that her brother had helped him into the house.

"Now, Miss Quinlan, did your father frequently remain away from home all night?"

Julia replied, "No, he sometimes was away 'til quite late at night but had no habit of staying away all night."

"As a general thing, I understand that the household work has been done by you since the death of your mother. Would that be correct?"

"'Twould."

"Can you speak of any trouble that ever arose either between you and your father or between your father and brother?"

"I know of no troubles like that."

"And as for money, did your father provide it when the two of you asked?"

"We were always given what spendin' money was asked for."

In cross-examination, the defense raised the matter of the turkey money and the dialogue became a little testy.

"Is it true that you had the money from the sale of any fowl you raised?"

"'Tis."

"Did you receive the money you had coming from your father for the sale of your turkeys on the 21st of December?"

"The day before his murder he paid me $40.57 from the sale of turkeys to Mr. Andrews."

"Was anyone else present when the turkey money was paid to you?"

"No."

"And there was no other arrangement between you and your father whereby you were to receive compensation for your labors at home?"

"No, and I didn't ask for any. I had no use or occasion for..."

"When your mother died, Miss Quinlan," interrupted the defense, waving documents before her eyes, "did she leave a bond and a mortgage against the homestead to you and your brother, Thomas?"

"Yes."

"They are in your possession now, correct?"

Julia acknowledged that the documents were hers and that nothing had ever been demanded or paid on the bond and mortgage. The defense attorney requested that the documents be offered in evidence.

The defense then asked if there had been anyone else at the house the night of the murder, in addition to her brother. Julia denied anyone else was present. She was asked to confirm that her father weighed about 210 pounds. She said that he did. Scratching his head, the lawyer said he found it hard to believe that her brother got a man of such weight into the wagon without assistance.

The defense, looking to see if Justice Smith was attending to his every word, then asked the witness, "Is it true that there is a man in addition to your brother working on your farm now?"

"'Tis so," responded Julia, who started nervously fidgeting with her hands.

"What is his name, please?"

"Morris O'Connors."

"And how long has he been working on your farm?" The question caused more fidgeting by the witness.

"A week after Pa's funeral Tom hired him to work on the farm, and he has stayed on since then."

"Was there any arrangement made with him to come and stay at the farm before the 21st of December?"

"No, there was no arrangement made until after harm was done to Pa."

"Are you certain, Miss Quinlan? Was Morris O'Connors at the farm in November, say around Thanksgiving time?"

"Yes, but...."

"Thank you, Miss Quinlan. You may step down."

The time was 4:40 p.m. when Frank Corl took the witness chair. His deposition of April 26 was read and acknowledged. He stated that neither McDonald nor Clark were present after dressing the turkeys when there was talk concerning the amount of money the turkeys brought. Then the examination was adjourned until Saturday morning.

15

Witnesses for the Defense

June 1, 1895:

The Quinlan murder case reopened at 8:50 Saturday morning with the reading of depositions made earlier by a host of individuals: Jerry Sullivan, O. P. Carlon, Alex H. Stewart, Josie Corl, Daniel Donahue, William Huttleston, and Cora E. Godfrey. Cross-examination of these witnesses was waived by McDonald's attorney.

At this point the plaintiff rested. McDonald was informed by Justice Smith that he as the Defendant had a right to make a statement according to Section 196 of the Code of Civil Procedure. McDonald waived the right to make such a statement. The defendant was not going to take the stand in his own defense. Others would be called by the defense instead.

The next witness to be called was Homer's black barber, the 62 year old William Jones. Jones testified that he knew Patrick Quinlan and first heard of his injury on that Saturday. He said he cut Quinlan's hair the night before. He thought the time was a bit

past 8 PM. He said he did not smell Quinlan's breath and that he did not seem to be intoxicated. The man was only in his shop for ten minutes, paid his bill, and left. No one else was in the shop at the time, and he did not see McDonald that night.

Twenty-nine year old Darius Ripley, a strapping carriage painter of Homer residing at 3 Allen Place, was summoned next. He had been a resident of Homer for the past twenty-six years. He had known McDonald for about eight years and Louis Clark for twelve years. He had heard of the Quinlan incident on Saturday afternoon shortly after 5 o'clock. Friday evening, December 21st, Ripley had spent at home and at The Brunswick saloon.

"I was at The Brunswick from 7 to 9:30 that evening. McDonald and Clark came in about the same time -- around 8:45. They stayed five minutes…possibly ten. I don't remember anyone else being in the barroom except another employee, Mr.Kenfield."

"Did McDonald and Clark leave The Brunswick together?"

"I reckon I can't say that they did or not."

"Did McDonald or Clark have any drinks at The Brunswick?"

"Again, I can't say that they got any drink there."

"So how can you be certain in your recollection that McDonald and Clark were even at The Brunswick?"

"It was the topic of discussion that Saturday at The Brunswick, and Kenfield brought it to my attention. On December 21st, he -- Kenfield -- was on one side of the bar and McDonald on the other. Kenfield asked McDonald who the tall one was, and he told him it was Clark."

"How soon after McDonald and Clark left The Brunswick did you leave?"

"I was in the saloon probably a good half hour after they went out. I was waitin' around for the show to open upstairs at Keator's. But I didn't end up goin' to the show. I went home instead. The show commenced about half an hour before I left."

Having established the defendant's location the night of the crime, the defense attorney had the carriage painter step down. In his place, Attorney Dickinson called for Mr. Lucius L. Clark. It was recorded that he was 60 years old, was a house and carriage painter living on King Street in the village, and was the father of Louis Clark who turned 25 last December.

"Mr. Clark, I understand you recently did some investigating into the Quinlan case of your own. Could you describe for the Court what you did and what you found?"

"Last Monday I went on foot from Homer to where Quinlan's body was said to have been found. I went up the Giles Road [now Creal Road] past Eldridge's for the purpose of seein' how long it would take to walk up and back. I may have walked a little faster than ordinarily. I started from my home and walked to the corner of James and Main Street. That took me twenty minutes. To go from my home to where Quinlan was and return took me one hour and fifteen minutes."

"So by your calculations, would you say that it takes under one hour and fifty-five minutes to go by foot from the corner of James and Main up to where Quinlan was found and back?"

"Yes, that's right."

"And how high would you figure the screen wire fence to be that is near the school ground spoken of yesterday?"

"I should say it's three and a half to four feet high."

"While you were at the spot where Quinlan's body was found, were you able to detect any sounds coming from the Quinlan house?"

"That I did. From that spot I could distinctly hear voices at the Quinlans'."

"Did you make any other observations while at that spot?"

"That I did. I walked about five or six rods beyond where Quinlan was found, and I paced across the road. I found it to be 21 feet from the board fence to the bank on the west side." Glancing to where Thomas Quinlan was seated, Mr. Clark concluded, "It looked to me as though a wagon could be turned around there anywhere near where poor Quinlan was found."

The defense had Morris Sullivan called to the stand next. He was a carriage painter by trade and the twenty year old son of Daniel Sullivan. He lived in Homer all his life and had known McDonald for around five years and Louis Clark for about three years. He first learned of Quinlan's death on the Sunday morning after. He was asked to remember the night of Quinlan's injury.

"On Friday night I was around the village of Homer from about six to nine o'clock. Between six and seven o'clock I saw McDonald and Clark at Murphy's. I saw them again near Reider's jewelry store [15 South Main] at about 9 o'clock. They were going toward Murphy's saloon [33 South Main], and I did not see them again. Before I saw them, I met several other persons on the street, but I don't remember whom. From Randall's saloon I went home with three or four other fellows. I got home, I would say, about twenty-five minutes past 9 o'clock."

"When you met McDonald and Clark at 9 PM were they under the influence of liquor?"

"I'm sorry; I can't recall whether they were or not."

All eyes turned upon the next witness called on the part of the defendant – Louis Clark. Arrested in Syracuse and charged along with McDonald with the murder of Patrick Quinlan, Clark took the stand.

16

The Other Charged with the Crime Testifies

Louis Clark, charged with the murder of Patrick Quinlan, gave his age as 25 and his occupation as carriage painter.

"When did you first know of Patrick Quinlan's injuries?"

"It was Saturday night when my attention was first called to the matter," Clark responded confidently.

"Do you know the defendant seated over here?"

Clark looked toward the defendant and answered, "Yes, that is 'Jack' McDonald, and I've known him five or six years now…perhaps longer."

"Were you in Mr. McDonald's company the night of December 21st?"

"Yes. I met him at about 6 o'clock on that Friday evening and was with him all the evening except for a few minutes near 7 when I left him. Then, I saw him again at Murphy's and I was with him the remainder of the evening until we retired for the night."

"Did you stay together through the night?"

"Yes."

"Did either of you leave the village of Homer that night after 7 o'clock?"

"No, sir, we did not." Again, the voice was confident.

"Were either of you in Doyle's that evening?"

"We both were."

"Did you know Patrick Quinlan?"

"No, sir. I never saw the man… that I know of."

"Did you hear anything said in Doyle's that night about turkeys or turkey money?"

"No, not a thing. I have no knowledge of Quinlan having sold any turkeys or receiving any money for them."

"Do you know where Patrick Quinlan lived outside of Homer?"

"I did not know at the time where Quinlan lived, and I would not know now except for hearing it here in court."

"Now is it true that you said in Doyle's that 'It's time we were going if we are going up there.'?"

"I don't remember sayin' any such thing. And if such a remark was made, it was not said in connection with Quinlan."

"I see. Could you tell the court what time it was when you and Mr. McDonald got back to Murphy's that night to turn in for the night?"

"Sorry, I can't tell you. You see, I was a little tipsy that night. I knew what was going on and all, but I was sick…vomited there."

"Yes, yes. Now, in regards to Mr. Fred Graham… did he, too, spend the night with you and Mr. McDonald?"

"Yes. We found Fred at Murphy's."

"Now Mr. Clark, could you please explain how you came to spend the night at Mr. McDonald's rooms at Murphy's?"

"Well, when I went out of Murphy's, I was quite sick, and 'Jack' asked me where I was goin'. I said I was goin' home. 'Jac' asked me to stay with him, knowin' how much my folks were opposed to drinkin'. So I did. There was no other motive. I didn't undress; I just lay on the sofa all night."

"And you never left at any time during the night?"

"Well, not exactly. During the night I got sicker. I called for something to vomit in and someone opened the door for me and I went out on the porch to throw up. I don't recall if the door was locked or not or who opened it for me."

"You have already given testimony at the coroner's inquest on January 1st, correct?"

"Yes and signed it as evidence."

"And it should be pointed out that you, at no time, have made an effort to evade the law. Is that correct?"

"Yes."

"Since being confined in jail, have you had any conversation with the defendant?"

"No. He's on one side of the corridor and I'm on the other."

"Have you ever been arrested before or charged with any other crime?"

"No."

Under cross-examination by the prosecution, certain inconsistencies were pointed out to the court. Clark claimed he was just as familiar with his whereabouts as reported by him at the inquest as now. Yet, he said he did not know that he had sworn to having told his mother on that Saturday morning that he had stayed in Cortland the night before. He could not swear that he was in Murphy's saloon at 9 o'clock. He denied that he had testified before the coroner that it was half past ten when he went into McDonald's room. He said he could not swear for sure that Murphy was in his saloon at all between half past 8 to 10 o'clock, but he thought he was.

The prosecution pressed him further. "On the night of December 21, 1894, Mr. Clark, after you left Doyle's at 7 o'clock, please trace your movements for the court."

"After Doyle's I was in The Brunswick saloon, then Donahue's, and Murphy's with McDonald."

"Are you absolutely certain you went no other place?"

"Yes," Clark responded with a raised voice. "I was in no other place in Homer that night except those three places after I left Doyle's."

"And you think that you and the defendant spent all the rest of the night in bed?"

Again, sounding miffed with this line of questioning, Clark adamantly retorted, "Yes, I think so. Except for those three saloons, after leaving Doyle's, I was asleep."

"Were you wearing narrow toed shoes that night?"

"No," Clark answered emphatically, "I wore broad toe shoes that night."

"So was either Mr. McDonald or Mr. Salisbury wearing pointed shoes that night?"

"Neither one of them had on pointed shoes that night."

"One more question, please. Do you recall hearing Patrick Quinlan at Doyle's saying 'It's after 8 o'clock and time for me to go.'?"

Practically glaring at the examiner, Clark rejoined, "I never heard any old man say 'It's after 8 o'clock and time for me to go.'"

"No other questions, your Honor."

It was 12:15 and an adjournment for dinner was taken until 1:45. At that time Darius Ripley was recalled by the defense. He wished to testify that he was mistaken about seeing McDonald and Clark at The Brunswick at 8:30 the night of December 21st. He had seen them there but on a night when Mr. Kenfield was present, and Kenfield had since told him that he was away from The Brunswick that night until after 11 o'clock.

"Thank you, Mr. Ripley, for clarifying that," said the defense, who immediately proceeded to call twenty-two year old Bert Darrow to the stand. Darrow said he saw Mike Murphy at the show at Keator's that night. The show was out at 10 PM, and George Paddock was with Murphy. He, also, thought he had seen McDonald and Clark in Kinney's place that night.

Forty-five year old Homer resident Melvin Chapman testified next. He was asked about his connection with Constable Shirley as regarding the Quinlan case.

"Mr. Shirley employed me to help find the murderer."

"How much did Constable Shirley pay you?"

"A dollar or a dollar and a half to begin with."

"What exactly were you to do for this pay?"

"I was to play cards with him and get him drunk."

"And did you?"

"I took him home two nights and he took me home one night. I was with McDonald four or five days, most of the time at The Inkstand."

Chapman stepped down, and E. B. Kenfield, thirty-three year old manager of The Brunswick in the Keator Block came forward.

"I was in Syracuse on December 21st. Came home on the 11:08 PM train. I know it was that day because that was the day I paid J. H. Doolittle some money. I had seen McDonald around but never saw Clark to know him until today. I heard of Pat Quinlan's injury on that Saturday but I can't remember who told me."

Kenfield's bartender, Nelson Crance, was called next. He corroborated his boss's testimony about being in Syracuse all day Friday.

"I think McDonald and Clark were in the place a few moments between 6 and 7 o'clock. I remember McDonald wanted to be trusted for drinks but I refused. To my recollection they were not in the place again that evening. But a few days after that McDonald came in and asked me if I remembered what time it was when he was there on Friday. I told him I did not. He said that it might make a difference with him if I could remember."

17

Sufficient Grounds for a Grand Jury Trial

June 1, 1895:

In cross-examination, the prosecution asked, "Mr. Crance, are you acquainted with Mr. Louis Clark?"

"No, I only know his brother J. D."

"Have you had any conversation about Louis with his brother?"

"I presume I told him some time last week that I did not know Louis."

"Was that true?"

"Well, yes, I did not know him then. I know who he is now."

"Good. Then could you now point out for the court the stranger you saw with Mr. McDonald at The Brunswick on the Friday in question?"

Crance turned with outstretched arm and pointed at Louis Clark seated at a table.

The prosecution stated, "Let the record show the witness identified the defendant, Louis Clark," and he returned to his seat.

John O'Connor testified next that he knew both McDonald and Clark. The thirty-year old was an employee of the Cortland Wagon Company who tended bar for Murphy on occasion.

"Murphy asked me to tend bar that night. He wanted to go to the show at the Opera House. I worked until 11 o'clock."

"Was the defendant and Mr. Clark there that night?"

"I did not see them in the saloon that night while I was there. I know they did not get drinks from me while I was there. In fact, I do not remember but four persons being served while I was there."

"What about in the side room?"

"I saw no one in the side room between 9 and 10 o'clock, but I can't swear no one was in there." With a smirk he added, "I know for sure there were no women comin' in while I was there." This comment brought forth some chuckles from court observers.

"Did you see or hear Mr. McDonald and Mr. Clark come in and go upstairs?"

"Well, I know they didn't come in and go through the bar room. Like I said, I don't remember seein' them at all that night. There are back stairs leading from the alleyway to the sleeping rooms, but I could not have heard anybody going up these stairs from the bar room."

"Now, Mr. O'Connor, think carefully. When you first came into the bar room that evening,, who was there?"

"I remember Bobby Owen was in there…."

"And McDonald and Clark?" interjected the attorney.

"They might have been there when I first went in, but I didn't see them."

Fred S. Owen was called to testify next. He offered what seemed to be a well-rehearsed statement.

"I live in Homer. I am 45 years old, and I am a carriage painter. I was in Murphy's from around 6 to 9 o'clock the evening of December 21st. O'Connor was there. McDonald and Clark were there between 7 and 8 o'clock. It must have been a little after 8 when they left. I can't say if O'Connor was there then. They were there from seven to ten minutes and then went out, and I didn't see them after that."

Representing the People, Attorney J. Courtney, Jr., then offered in evidence portions of the evidence given by Louis Clark before Coroner Bradford last December, and adjournment was taken until Monday morning.

June 3, 1895:

Attorney Smith summed up, as the newspaper put it, "in his usual able manner" for defendant McDonald. He was followed in the afternoon by prosecuting attorney Courtney's "very clear and comprehensive statement of the case."

Immediately after Courtney concluded his summation, the trial of the People vs. Louis Clark was called. Twenty-six depositions taken by Justice Smith prior to issuing warrants for the arrest of McDonald and Clark were read. Testimony was offered by Sheriff Adam Hillsinger. He stated that he knew defendant Clark and heard him make a statement on that Saturday morning concerning his whereabouts on the evening of December 21st and the morning of December 22nd. Adjournment was then called.

June 4, 1895:

Examination of Sheriff Hillsinger resumed with his testimony.

"The statement I heard Clark make was during the giving of his testimony on the examination of John McDonald. I heard him say that he was with McDonald from 6 or 7 in the evening of December 21st until the following morning."

The statement was reduced to writing by the Court and signed by Clark and read in evidence. With that the People rested, and the Defense offered in evidence the testimony of the witnesses for the defense in the trial of McDonald. The People then offered in evidence the testimony of these witnesses upon cross-examination.

The Defense then moved for the discharge of Clark on the ground of insufficient evidence to hold him for appearance before the grand jury. The motion was denied. The Court decided to hold McDonald as principal and Clark as accomplice. The two were remanded to jail. The crime for which McDonald was being held was not subject to bail, but Clark's bail was fixed at $1,000 even though the DA insisted it should be at least $10,000. The next grand jury was set to sit in October.

June 5, 1895:

The *Cortland Evening Standard* reported that the discrepancy between McDonald and Clark regarding bail "has caused some comment as being, to the lay observer, a little illogical." The paper went on to say: "As Clark testified that he was with McDonald the whole of the night or period during which the crime is charged to have been committed, it would seem either both should be held alike, or both discharged, for the penal code has destroyed the distinction between principal and accomplices by declaring that all who participate, aid or abet in the commission of a crime are principals." The paper cited a case in Syracuse where two were sentenced to death for a murder though only one did the shooting and the other was merely an accomplice.

July, 1895:

McDonald's counsel appeared in Canastota, New York, before Judge Gerret A. Forbes to request that McDonald be admitted to bail in accordance with Sections 552 and 558 of the code of criminal procedure. Appeal was based on the grounds that the evidence was not sufficient for holding the prisoner in jail. District Attorney Burlingame opposed the motion, and Judge Forbes denied the motion. McDonald remained incarcerated without bail.

18

Verdict of the Grand Jury

October 18, 1895:

The grand jury convened in the fall of 1895 in the case of John McDonald. Almost ten months to the day of the crime, the grand jury reached a verdict. On October 18, 1895, the jury voted almost unanimously for acquittal. It failed to find an indictment against John McDonald for the murder of Patrick Quinlan, and he was discharged. By order of the committing magistrate, the DA was precluded from presenting to the grand jury the case of Louis Clark, the alleged accomplice.

The local paper reported: "Perhaps no case which has been before the grand jury in some time has roused more general interest than that of John McDonald charged with the murder of Patrick Quinlan. The district attorney and the county officers made a very thorough, searching and painstaking examination and followed to the end every clue that could be furnished."

Whoever murdered Patrick Quinlan remained at large and was never identified and brought to justice.

Main St., Homer, N. Y.

This case proves you can get away with murder – at least in Homer back in 1894-95. Who did it and for what motive? Was it John McDonald or Louis Clark in a case of robbery? Was it a family member resentful of restrictive living or financial circumstances on the Quinlan farm? Thomas Quinlan? Julia Quinlan? Or was it a patron of one of an abundance of saloons in the village? If you think all of the drinking spots in the village played a role in this case, you would be mistaken. The Mansion House owned by J. H. Day on South Main [where the fire station is located today] was apparently not frequented by any of the figures in the story, unless that is where The Inkstand saloon was ensconced in some corner. Or was the perpetrator of the homicide someone else in the community that jumped Patrick Quinlan for his cash or for some other reason a few days before Christmas? What if it was someone who had patronized George I. Pruden's photography studio at 8 South Main in Homer? That means there may be a "mug shot," so to speak, of the culprit out there lurking in someone's attic or family album. What if Julia Quinlan had married Morris O'Connors, the man who was at the Quinlan farm the last months of 1894? Would that cast suspicion upon the two of them? Evidence of such a marriage has not been found. The 1910 U. S. Census shows Thomas Quinlan to be the "Head of Household" in Homer and Julia to be still residing there as "Sister." Neither one of them had married sixteen years after the murder, and any motive for collusion is too weak. That, of course, does not remove the mysterious Mr. O'Connors from the list of possible perpetrators of the crime.

The Quinlan murder remains a "cold case." How would the case have turned out had it occurred today? Given modern technology and forensic science that can now be brought to bear in criminal cases, how would the case have been handled differently and the perpetrator of the crime brought to justice? Certainly, access to the crime scene would have been restricted and evidence would not be tampered with as it was then. At least one fact continues through time in the American legal system: You are innocent until proven guilty, and you better secure a seasoned attorney.

Finally, it needs to be stated that there is only one thing more disappointing and frustrating than reading a murder mystery that concludes with justice denied, and that is doing research on a case that leaves the researcher hanging instead of the murderer. I apologize to the reader for a story that does not go anywhere. History, unlike fiction, does that sometimes. I recognize that the story lends itself to an expanded, colorful novel in which the murderer(s) get caught, justice prevails, and the reader comes away feeling satisfied, but that project must be left for another day.

For now, this narrative ends with the question: Whom do you say murdered Patrick Quinlan on the longest night of 1894?

Photograph Credits

Page 3: 1876 Homer Atlas Map – lots 33 and 34 show the home of Patrick Quinlan (collection of CCHS)

Page 4 (upper right hand corner): Christmas Greeting Card (collection of Martin Sweeney)

Page 4 (center): Christmas Greeting Card (collection of CCHS)

Page 5: James Street in Homer, then and now (courtesy of Homer Town Archives)

Page 6: Homer Train Depot, 1905 (collection of Martin Sweeney)

Page 7: Looking west on James Street from the Barber Block, 1908, this would be the path that Quinlan would have taken on December 22, 1894 (collection of Martin Sweeney)

Page 11: Photo of a horse-pulled trolley (courtesy of Homer Town Archives)

Page 17: Andrew's store on Main Street, in the Brockway Block (collection of Martin Sweeney)

Page 26: Main Street, Homer, 1908 (courtesy of Homer Town Archives)

Page 40: Invitation to a dance at the Hotel Windsor, 1899 (collection of Martin Sweeney)

Page 44: Electric trolley (collection of Martin Sweeney)

Page 48: Photograph of advertisement for Sig Sautelle's Circus (collection of CCHS)

Page 49: Cortland County Courthouse (collection of CCHS)

Page 54: Dr. George W. Bradford, Physician & Coroner (collection of CCHS)

Page 67: Fr. John J. McLoughlin (1894) from an 1897 Christmas booklet for St. Mary's Church, Cortland, NY (courtesy of Mary Ann Kane)

Page 80: Homer Green, 1907 (collection of Martin Sweeney)

Page 87: North side of Main Street Looking South (collection of CCHS)

Page 91: Ad for Homer Manufacturing Company in *The Carriage Monthly*, 1894 (collection of Martin Sweeney)

Page 102: Main Street, with Trolley (collection of Martin Sweeney)

18703800R00060

Made in the USA
Charleston, SC
17 April 2013